AGA
easy

AGA easy

LUCY YOUNG

A.
Absolute Press

First published in Great Britain in 2006 by Absolute Press. This paperback edition first published in paperback in 2009 by

Absolute Press
Scarborough House
29 James Street West
Bath BA1 2BT
Phone 44 (0) 1225 316013
Fax 44 (0) 1225 445836
E-mail info@absolutepress.co.uk
Website www.absolutepress.co.uk

Publisher Jon Croft
Commissioning Editor Meg Avent
Designer Matt Inwood
Publishing Assistant Meg Devenish
Photographer Philip Webb
Food Stylist Joss Herd
Props Stylist Cynthia Inions

A catalogue record of this book is available from the British Library

ISBN: 9781906650087

Printed and bound on behalf of Latitude Press in Slovenia.

A note about the text
This book is set in Helvetica Neue. Helvetica was designed in 1957 by Max Miedinger of the Swiss-based Haas foundry. In the early 1980s, Linotype redrew the entire Helvetica family. The result was Helvetica Neue.

contents

introduction

I have loved writing this book! It it has given me the wonderful opportunity to create easy recipes for the home cook, helping make life in the kitchen less stressful.

During the past sixteen years I have been working alongside Mary Berry, both running, and teaching the Aga workshops. I now know an Aga inside out and can honestly say there really is no cooker like it. It was a real thrill when finally two years ago I bought my own. At last my passion for Aga cooking could extend to home as well as at work.

An Aga is the heart of any kitchen – often said and very true. Whether you live in a cottage in the country or a modern loft in the city, the Aga has the ability to turn any kind of house into a home. These recipes are written for the home cook, simple to cook, yet full of flavour. Perfect for serving to family and friends.

The Aga, of course, cooks roasts and casseroles brilliantly – and there are recipes in the book for these, but I've also included many contemporary recipes, which can be cooked just as successfully on the Aga. In fact there is really nothing you can't cook well on the Aga, all you need to do is learn a few simple techniques and it will soon become a doddle! My style of cooking is very much about enjoying a calm kitchen and being a laid-back type of cook. Spending hours in the kitchen only to serve a meal you are too exhausted to eat is not my idea of fun. Cooking should be a pleasure for everyone, both for you and your guests.

For each recipe I have stated how many people it will serve and whether or not it can be frozen. I've also included conventional oven techniques and timings.

I hope you enjoy these easy recipes, safe in the knowledge your family and friends are sure to be impressed.

So don't panic, stay calm and enjoy!

Lucy Young
July 2006

general information

All Agas are different, whether oil, gas, electric, each one is individual. For instance, even if you and your neighbour both have gas Agas you may find they don't behave the same. We are often asked at our Aga workshops which number we run our Aga on, this really doesn't matter, on yours it may be 2 on mine it may be 6 – the important thing is that the indicator is on or around the line. A converted Aga (one changed from solid fuel to a modern fuel) may have a cooler simmering oven as will an older Aga. Remember: Agas don't wear out. I demonstrated recently on a 60-year-old Aga and it was a star!

We always encourage readers to make notes in their recipe books – I think this is especially important when cooking with an Aga as timings may vary, so make notes as you go. This will be a great help when you come back to the same recipe again.

AGA hot plates
For all Agas the hot plates are the same, left is the boiling plate and right is the simmering plate. Keep the lids down as much as possible as this will conserve the heat and the ovens will function more efficiently.

2-oven AGA
The top oven is the roasting oven. It is extremely hot and has all round heat. Slide at the top for browning and directly onto the floor for frying and grilling. The floor of the roasting oven has very intense heat – treat it as an extra hot plate – perfect for baking pastry and cooking bacon. The bottom oven is the simmering oven, a cooler oven –perfect for slow cooking casseroles or baking meringues.

3-oven AGA
Very similar to the 2 oven Aga but has the baking oven bottom left. This oven is a medium heat and perfect for cakes and general cooking.

4-oven AGA
This has the roasting oven top right. Baking oven bottom right, simmering oven top left and warming oven bottom left. The warming oven is just that, it keeps food and plates warm, a very useful oven.

runners
When runners are mentioned in the recipes, these are counted from the top.

shelves
The grid shelves are the oven shelves which slide into the oven on the runners or directly onto the floor.

cold sheet/plain shelf
The cold sheet also known as the plain shelf is stored out of the oven and is used to blank off the heat and lower the temperature of the oven when something

is getting too brown. For example, if you are baking a quiche and it is golden brown on top but needs longer cooking in the centre, slide the cold sheet two sets of runners above, this will prevent if from getting too brown.

pots and pans

It is important to use good quality pans. I would recommend Aga branded products, these have been tried and tested on the Aga and can withstand the intense heat. It is important to have a ground-base to your pan as thin-based pans can buckle under the intense heat. Once buckled, they will lose contact with the hot plates and will take longer to boil. I would suggest buying a large non-stick frying pan, non-stick milk pan and some stainless steel medium-sized pans. Try and buy a range that can all be used in the ovens (with heatproof or removable handles). Pans should also have flat lids as these can be stacked in the ovens, making cooking much more efficient.

baking sheets and roasting tins

The Aga branded roasting tins and baking sheets are the best, they are made to fit the ovens and will slide along the runners. They can also withstand the intense temperature of the roasting oven. There are two sizes of roasting tins and baking sheets available, both fit on the runners of the oven. If you do have old tins or trays they are fine to use as long as they are flat and not too buckled.

cleaning

For general cleaning of the enamel surface and lids use a cream cleaner and a damp cloth, wipe again to remove any excess. Ecloths are very good, use them damp and wipe over the enamel surface and lids – they will not leave a smear. Constant wiping is important as this prevents any dirt becoming ingrained in the enamel. For really stubborn stains use Astonish or a well soaped Brillo pad. For the area around the plates (not on the enamel) use the wire brush supplied with your Aga. For cleaning under the lids, place the cold sheet flat on the plates (this prevents you from getting too hot) and use a damp Brillo to clean the insides. We do not clean the insides of the ovens, this is because once cleaned as soon as you close the door and begin cooking the inside will immediately turn black again – life's a bit too short for cleaning inside! Anything that has spilt onto the floor of the Aga will burn away, so no need to worry unless it turns to charcoal and then simply brush with the wire brush. Finally, finish with a spray of polish and wipe with a duster and this will give your Aga a wonderful shine.

servicing

Treat your Aga like you would your car – remember to service it regularly as recommended. This is so important to keep the Aga running smoothly. Be sure to have your authorised Aga engineer to service it, if you don't and anything major goes wrong Aga themselves will not touch it. Remember to turn your Aga off the night before servicing so that it cools down. The pilot light can stay on and the Aga technician will relight it for you before he leaves.

how to use this book

- All the eggs used are large.

- If the recipe says just 'flour' use plain flour. I state when to use self-raising flour.

- For all spoon measurements I have used measuring spoons to be accurate.

- Weigh in either imperial or metric but don't mix the two.

- If recipe says just 'oil' use sunflower oil or vegetable oil. I state when olive oil is best to use.

- If using double cream in a recipe, buy pouring double cream as it is easier to mix.

- For baking, use softened butter or a chilled vegetable fat such as Stork.

good things to know

- To get more juice out of a lemon or lime, heat in the simmering oven or warming oven for 15 minutes.

- Heat sugar for whisked sponges in the simmering or warming oven to give more volume quickly when whisked.

- If you are concerned when cooking meat to know when it is done, buy a meat thermometer and insert into the thickest part of the meat.

- For a glaze, or for icing cakes, heat jam in the jar on the enamel on the back of the Aga or in the simmering or warming oven – once warm it is easier to spread.

- If honey, syrup, treacle has gone hard in its tin heat in its tin on the enamel on the back of Aga or in the simmering or warming oven and it will turn runny.

- Preheat the Aga toaster before toasting to prevent the bread from sticking.

- Melt chocolate in a bowl on the enamel on the back of the Aga.

- Prove and rise bread in large sealed bags sitting on tea towels around the Aga.

- To open metal screw lids on jars, simply invert on the simmering plate for about 30 seconds to allow the metal to expand. Then, using a tea towel, remove the lid with ease.

- Invert empty serving dishes on the enamel tops around the Aga to heat.

- If cooking for a large group and you need to use a number of pans, check first that they will all fit into the oven together by placing them on the cold sheet – it's the same size as the oven.

success with AGA cooking

- Keep the cold sheet/plain shelf out of the oven so it stays cold and ready to use.

- Keep lids down as much as possible and cook in the ovens.

- Before casseroles go into the simmering oven, bring to the boil first.

- The floor of the roasting oven is exceedingly hot, ideal for browning the base of quiches or grilling bacon or roasting vegetables.

- Ensure the heat indicator is always on the line, this means your Aga is set at the right temperature – check first thing in the morning.

equipment

- Use pans with a thick ground base, the hot plates of the Aga have a very intense heat and if your pans are thin they will buckle and therefore be a poor conductor of heat.

- When cooking on the top plates use as wide a based pan as possible to cover the plates, so no heat is wasted.

- Bake-O-Glide or Lift Off paper, are non-stick silicone papers perfect for using in the oven or on the simmering plate for frying eggs, pizzas, meringues, etc.
- For really dirty roasting tins, soak overnight in dissolved biological powder.
- Use only wooden or Teflon utensils in non-stick pans – metal will damage the coating.

For more information on Lucy Young and Mary Berry visit **www.maryberry.co.uk**.

For more information on Aga visit **www.aga-web.co.uk** or **www.agalinks.com**.

easy
starters and
canapés

quick fish tapenade

Serve this tapenade with tiny pieces of Melba toast (see opposite) as a canapé or, just as lovely, as a dip with pitta bread as a starter. It can be made up to 2 days ahead.

❄ Not suitable for freezing.

4 anchovies fillets from a can in oil, drained
1 x 130g can tuna in oil, drained
100g (4oz) butter, cut into cubes
1 x 200g (7oz) tub full-fat cream cheese
juice of half a lemon
12 medium-sized pitted black olives, halved
1 good tablespoons chives, snipped
Pepper for seasoning

Measure all the ingredients into a processor and whiz until smooth. Turn into individual ramekins or a terrine dish.

Chill in the fridge for a minimum of an hour. Serve with snipped chives on top.

serves 6

classic melba toast

✽ Melba Toast freezes well when layered with kitchen towel in a poly box.

3 slices medium white bread

Preheat the Aga toaster on the boiling plate with the lid down. Put the bread in the toaster and toast until golden brown on each side. Cut off the crusts and cut through each slice horizontally. Remove any excess dough from the centre. Cut each slice diagonally into four triangles. Arrange on a baking sheet, uncooked side up.

Slide the baking sheet on to the floor of the roasting oven for about 5 minutes until the toasts are crisp and the edges curl. Alternatively, cook in the simmering oven for about 25 minutes until crisp and the edges curl.

makes 24 triangles

conventional oven
Toast the bread. Slide the triangles under a preheated medium grill for about 3–5 minutes until crisp and the edges curl.

baked vegetable crisps

Just like the ones you buy in supermarkets – only better! My favourites are carrot, sweet potato, squash, beetroot and parsnip. Store in a sealed plastic box lined with kitchen paper.

❄ These freeze well.

Slice the vegetables wafer-thin. You can also cut them into different shapes for variation. For example, parsnips look wonderful cut into long thin strips.

Arrange the slices in a single layer on a baking sheet lined with non-stick paper. Sprinkle generously with salt and slide into the simmering oven and cook for about $2\frac{1}{2}$–3 hours until dry and crisp.

If you make these ahead you may need to crisp them up on the floor of the roasting oven for about 2 minutes before serving.

Serve cold in a bowl.

conventional oven
Cook in a preheated oven 140C/120C Fan/Gas 2 for about 2 hours until crisp. If getting too brown switch the oven off and leave in the hot oven to dry out.

glazed honey and mustard mini sausages

I love these sausages; they are delicious served at any time and on any occasion – with the added bonus that children will adore them!

✳ Not suitable for freezing.

30 cocktail sausages
2 tablespoons Dijon mustard
2 tablespoons runny honey

Arrange the sausages in a small roasting tin. Slide the tin onto the second set of runners in the roasting oven for about 15 minutes. Mix the honey and mustard together in a small bowl. Pour the mustard and honey over the hot sausages and stir and shake to coat all the sausages.

Return to the second set of runners in the roasting oven for a further 5 minutes until sticky, golden brown and glossy.

makes 30

conventional oven
Cook the sausages under the grill until golden brown. Toss in the mustard and honey and return under the grill for a further 5 minutes.

special blinis

Blinis are brilliant and make such a versatile canapé because you can add pretty much any topping you like (see below for some suggestions).

❊ Blinis freeze well without the topping.

100g (4oz) flour
2 eggs
50ml (2floz) milk
little salt

Measure the ingredients into a bowl and whisk until you have a smooth, but fairly thick batter.

Lift the lid on the simmering plate for about 3–4 minutes to cool a little. Grease the plate with little oil on kitchen paper.

Spoon a teaspoon of the mixture directly onto the plate and cook until bubbles start to appear (about 30 seconds), flip over using a small palette knife and cook for a further 20 seconds until golden brown and cooked through.

makes about 20 blinis

conventional oven
Preheat a non-stick frying pan until piping hot, spoon a teaspoon of the mixture into the pan and cook for about a minute on each side or until bubble appear, turning over halfway through.

ideas for toppings
Cream cheese and smoked salmon
Horseradish and pastrami
Pesto, cherry tomato and Mozzarella
Curried mayonnaise and prawns
Parma ham and mango
Half hard-boiled quails egg and hollandaise sauce
Mango chutney and chorizo sausage

a simple salsa

This really is the simplest of simple salsas, both quick to prepare and perfect to serve. Try with pitta bread as a dip or as an accompaniment to grilled fish or burgers. Because this salsa is uncooked it is really important for all the ingredients to be cut to the same size. The salsa can be made up to 12 hours ahead.

❄ Not suitable for freezing

1 small red onion, very finely chopped
$1/2$ cucumber, seeds removed, very finely chopped
4 tomatoes, seeds removed, very finely chopped
1 tablespoon balsamic vinegar
1 tablespoon olive oil
1 tablespoon mango chutney
salt and pepper

Prepare all the ingredients and mix together in a bowl. Season with salt and pepper to taste.

Serve cold.

serves 4–6

spring onion and cucumber raita

Raitas are traditionally served with hot curries to temper the heat from the chillis. But I think the raita is such a versatile dish that it can be served with any number of meat and fish dishes or simply as a dip. My version is especially good with lamb burgers and kebabs. If making ahead, stir in the cucumber at the last minute to avoid the raita becoming too thin.

❄ Not suitable for freezing.

$^{1}/_{2}$ cucumber
4 spring onions, finely chopped
1 x 200g tub Greek yoghurt
2 tablespoons fresh mint, chopped
1 teaspoon of mint sauce
salt and pepper

Cut the cucumber lengthways and using a teaspoon, scoop out the seeds and discard. If the skin is very thick, remove it using a potato peeler, though I prefer to leave the skin on. Chop into tiny raisin size pieces and tip into a bowl.

Add the remaining ingredients to the cucumber and stir. Season with salt and pepper.

Serve cold.

serves 4–6

five spice pork with little gem

This is one of my favourite canapés, which can also be served as a starter or light lunch, with or without sour cream.

❄ Not suitable for freezing.

2 tablespoons oil
450g (1lb) lean minced pork
2cm (1") fresh ginger, peeled, grated
1 red chilli, finely chopped
6 spring onions, finely sliced
1 tablespoon Chinese five spice powder
3 tablespoons soy sauce
salt and pepper

plum sauce to serve
24 little gem-heart leaves
sour cream to serve

Heat the oil in a large non-stick frying pan on the boiling plate. Add the pork and fry, breaking up the mince with two wooden spoons as it's frying, until golden brown.

Add the ginger, chilli, onions, spice and soy and fry for a minute. Season with salt and pepper, cover and transfer to the simmering oven for about 30 minutes until the pork is cooked.

Arrange the gem leaves on a large platter, spoon half a teaspoon of plum sauce into each leaf and then place a teaspoon of pork mixture on top. Finish with a little blob of sour cream.

Serve immediately and eat with your fingers.

serves 6 (4 leaves per person)

conventional oven
Cook the pork covered over a low heat on the hob.

cheesy cauliflower soup

A very quick, thick and creamy soup packed full of rich flavours. Can be made up to 2 days ahead.

❄ Freezes well without cheese. To serve, defrost bring to the boil and add the cheese.

1 large (about 1$\frac{3}{4}$lb) cauliflower
1 onion, finely chopped
600ml (1 pint) milk
600ml (1 pint) chicken stock
salt and pepper
1 teaspoon of Dijon mustard
75g (3oz) farmhouse Cheddar cheese, grated
2 tablespoons fresh parsley, chopped

Remove the florets from the cauliflower and cut them so they are even in size. Peel the stalk and cut into small chunks.

Put the cauliflower florets and stalks, onion, milk and stock into a large saucepan, bring to the boil on the boiling plate and boil for about 2 minutes. Cover and transfer to the simmering oven for about 15 minutes until the cauliflower is just tender.

Carefully spoon into a processor or blender and whiz until smooth. Pour back into the saucepan, season with salt and pepper and bring to the boil. Add the mustard and cheese, stirring all the time until the cheese has melted and the soup is hot.

Serve hot garnished with parsley.

serves 4–6

conventional oven
Gently simmer on the hob for about 15 minutes, until the cauliflower is tender.

a hearty winter soup

The addition of macaroni helps make this a really comforting and warming soup on a cold winter's day.

❇ Not suitable for freezing.

3 small sticks celery, cut into tiny dice
1 large carrot, peeled cut into tiny dice
1 onion, finely chopped
$1/2$ small pointed cabbage, shredded very finely
2 x 400g (14oz) tins of chopped tomatoes
1.2 litre (2 pints) vegetable stock
50g (2oz) macaroni pasta
$2^{1}/_{2}$ tablespoons green pesto.

Measure all the ingredients, except the pesto into a deep saucepan. Bring to the boil on the boiling plate and boil for a couple of minutes.

Cover and transfer to the simmering oven for about 30 minutes, until the vegetables are just tender and the macaroni is cooked, season with salt and pepper. Stir in the pesto and serve immediately.

serves 6–8

conventional oven
Simmer over a low heat for about 35 minutes until tender.

chaweng noodle soup

A healthy and delicious soup with an oriental flavour. Can be made ahead but add the noodles just before serving.

❄ Not suitable for freezing.

1 tablespoon olive oil
175g (6oz) button mushrooms, thinly sliced
8 spring onions, sliced, keeping white and green parts separate
about 3cm (1$\frac{1}{2}$ inches) fresh ginger, peeled and grated
1.2 litres (2 pints) vegetable stock
2 teaspoons fish sauce
2 teaspoons brown sugar
150g (5oz) fresh, cooked small prawns
salt and pepper
100g (4oz) fine egg noodles
2 small red chillies, cut in half lengthways through the stem, seeds removed,
    to garnish

Heat the oil in a saucepan on the boiling plate. Add the mushrooms, whites of the spring onions and the ginger. Stir, very quickly and add the stock, fish sauce and sugar, bring to the boil, stirring, add the prawns and green parts of the spring onions. Season with salt and pepper.

Cook the noodles according to packet instructions, drain and divide between 4 deep bowls. Spoon over the soup and serve hot with half a red chilli floating on the top of each bowl for garnish.

serves 4

conventional oven
Cook on the hob.

portabella mushroom with pesto and asparagus

I like to serve these mushrooms as a starter, one per person, or with a dressed salad as a light supper dish. I use full size asparagus tips for this recipe, not the fine ones often sold in supermarkets. Buy same-thickness mushrooms. Peppadew peppers are delicious sweet bell peppers, bought in a jar, mild or hot – I use the mild ones.

❄ Not suitable for freezing

4 large Portabella mushrooms
salt and pepper
a little olive oil
4 teaspoons of green pesto
6 Peppadew peppers, cut into thin strips
12 asparagus tips
2 tablespoons of fresh Parmesan, finely grated
a little balsamic vinegar

Carefully remove the stalks from the mushrooms, ensuring they stay whole. Brush each side of the mushroom with a little oil and season with salt and pepper. Heat a large non-stick frying pan on the boiling plate and fry the mushrooms for about 3 minutes on each side until lightly browned (if thin they may take only 2 minutes on each side). Arrange gill-side up on a baking sheet.

Cook the asparagus tips in boiling salted water for about 3 minutes until al dente. Drain and refresh in cold water.

Mix the pesto with the peppadew strips in a bowl and spoon over the gill-side of each mushroom. Arrange three asparagus tips on top of each mushroom. Sprinkle Parmesan over the asparagus. Slide onto the grid shelf on the floor of the roasting oven for about 6–8 minutes until piping hot and the Parmesan has melted.

Serve hot, drizzled with a little balsamic vinegar.

serves 4

best-ever stuffed red peppers

These brilliantly retro stuffed peppers with a modern twist are great as an al fresco dinner party starter, or as a supper dish simply accompanied with a dressed herb salad. For a subtle variation in taste and texture you could substitute Parma ham or Serrano ham for the Blackforest ham.

❄ Not suitable for freezing.

2 red peppers
4 teaspoons sun-dried tomato paste
1 x 125g tub full-fat cream cheese
salt and pepper
1 tablespoon fresh thyme leaves
4 large slices Blackforest Ham
4 teaspoons Balsamic vinegar

Quarter each pepper through the stem and remove the seeds. Sit the peppers on a baking sheet and season with salt and pepper.

Spread each pepper quarter with half a teaspoon of sun-dried tomato paste. Spoon a good teaspoon of cream cheese on top and sprinkle with salt and pepper and fresh thyme leaves. Cut each slice of ham in half and twist each slice and sit on top of the cheese.

Slide onto the floor of the roasting oven for about 12–15 minutes until the ham is crispy and piping hot.

Pour half a teaspoon of balsamic vinegar over each pepper and serve hot with dressed rocket leaves.

serves 4 (two per person)

conventional oven
Bake in a preheated oven 200C/180C Fan/Gas 6 for about 15 minutes until crispy and piping hot.

retro prawn and smoked salmon cocktail

The prawn cocktail is back! I have added smoked salmon to my version. If you are short of time buy cooked tiger prawns and add the lemon zest and juice to the sauce.

❄ Not suitable for freezing.

$1/2$ small iceberg lettuce, very finely shredded
a good knob of butter
225g (8oz) raw tiger prawns, without head or shell
zest and juice of half a lemon
salt and pepper
3 tablespoons low-fat mayonnaise
1 tablespoon tomato ketchup
1 tablespoon creamed horseradish
2 tablespoons fresh dill, chopped
6 smoked salmon cocktail slices, trimmed to any oblong shape

Arrange 6 x 7cm ($2^3/_4$") cooking rings on a baking sheet or plate. Push the shredded lettuce into the base of each ring.

Heat the butter in a non-stick frying pan, add the prawns and fry on the boiling plate for a couple of minutes until bright pink and cooked, turning over halfway through. Sprinkle the lemon zest and juice over the prawns. Season with salt and pepper and set aside to cool.

Measure the mayonnaise, ketchup, horseradish and dill into a mixing bowl, mix together and season with salt and pepper. Add in the prawns and stir until coated. Chop any of the trimmings from the smoked salmon and stir into the prawn mixture. Spoon the mixture on top of the lettuce, pressing the prawns into the rings.

Take a slice of smoked salmon and curl it on top of the prawns so it is sitting high.

To serve, squeeze a wedge of lemon over the top and grind with black pepper.

serves 6

rise-again goats' cheese and parma ham soufflés

The 'twice-baked soufflé' was invented many years ago by my great friend and colleague Mary Berry. For this recipe you make the soufflés in advance and then arrange them in a dish with the sauce, ready to pop in the oven 15 minutes before serving! The easiest soufflés in the world!

❋ To freeze: wrap the soufflés in clingfilm after the first baking and freeze individually.

40g (1½ oz) butter
40g (1½ oz) flour
300ml (½ pint) milk
1 teaspoon Dijon mustard
salt and pepper
3 eggs, separated
1 x 150g (5oz) pot creamy goats' cheese
50g (2oz) Parma ham, snipped into pieces
2 tablespoons fresh basil, chopped

sauce
150ml (¼ pint) pouring double cream
2 good teaspoons of sundried tomato paste
25g (1oz) mature cheddar, grated
chopped basil to garnish

You will need 6 x size 1 ramekins, buttered and base lined with a disc of non-stick paper.

Melt the butter in a wide-based saucepan on the boiling plate. Off the heat, whisk in the flour and return to the boiling plate. Gradually blend in the milk, whisking continuously until the sauce boils. Stir in the mustard and season with salt and pepper.

Add the egg yolks to the white sauce. Stir in the goats' cheese, Parma ham and basil. Whisk the egg whites until stiff. Carefully cut and fold the egg whites into the mixture until smooth.

Spoon the mixture evenly into the ramekins and sit them in a small roasting tin. Pour boiling water into the tin until it comes halfway up the sides of the ramekins. Slide the tin onto the grid shelf on the floor of the roasting oven for about 15–20 minutes, until the soufflés are well-risen and lightly golden brown. You may need to slide the cold sheet onto the second set of runners if getting too brown. Once cooked, set aside to cool in the ramekins.

Mix the tomato paste with the cream and season with salt and pepper. Pour into a shallow ovenproof dish. Carefully remove the soufflés from the ramekins, remove the disc of paper and arrange brown side up, on top of the sauce. Sprinkle cheese over the top.

To serve: reheat on the grid shelf on the floor of the roasting oven for about 15–20 minutes until risen again and piping hot.

Serve hot with a dressed salad.

serves 6

conventional oven
Cook in preheated oven 220C/200C Fan/Gas 7 for 15–20 minutes until golden. To reheat for serving, bake at the same temperature in a preheated oven for 15–20 minutes.

king prawns
with garlic and chilli

A great party dish. When cooked, tip the prawns into a large bowl and leave your guests to dig in. Be sure to have an extra bowl on the table for the discarded shells as well as finger bowls and napkins, it can get messy!

❋ Not suitable for freezing.

16 raw king prawns, with head and shell

marinade
2 small red chillies, deseeded and chopped very finely
3 cloves garlic, crushed
Juice of half a lemon
2 tablespoons olive oil
3 tablespoons fresh parsley, chopped

Arrange the prawns in a single layer in a dish. Measure ingredients for the marinade into a bowl and pour over the prawns. Marinate for a minimum of 30 minutes in the fridge.

Tip the prawns into a large roasting tin so they lie in a single layer. Slide the tin onto the floor of the roasting oven for about 8 minutes. Turn the prawns over half way through and cook till piping hot and bright pink.

Tip the prawns and juices into a serving bowl, sprinkle over chopped parsley and serve hot with crusty chunky bread.

serves 4

conventional oven
Roast the prawns in a preheated oven 200C/180C Fan/Gas 6 or under the grill for about 8 minutes until bright pink and piping hot.

warm goats' cheese and pear salad

A really lovely summer lunch dish or easy dinner party starter. The pear and cheese combination is one made in culinary heaven. The salad plates can be prepared in advance and the goats' cheese just popped in the oven for a few minutes prior to serving.

❄ Not suitable for freezing.

1 x 100g (4oz) firm goats' cheese in a roll, rind on
a little olive oil
2 tablespoons of fresh rosemary, finely chopped
1 x 70g bag rocket
2 ripe pears, peeled and thinly sliced
12 small radishes, quartered

mustard dressing
1 tablespoon grainy mustard
2 tablespoons white wine vinegar
6 tablespoons olive oil
1 good teaspoon caster sugar

Remove the end rind from the goats' cheese, leaving the outer rind on. Cut the cheese into three even slices. Brush each side of cheese with a little oil. Press rosemary onto each side of the slices. Arrange on non-stick paper on a baking sheet.

Divide the rocket between six small plates. Scatter pears and radishes around the rocket on each plate. Whisk all the ingredients for the dressing in a small bowl and season with salt and pepper.

Slide the baking sheet with the goats' cheese onto the top set of runners in the roasting oven for about 3 minutes. Using a fish slice carefully place one slightly melted cheese round on top of the salad. Spoon over a little dressing and serve.

serves 6

conventional oven
Slide the goats' cheese under a medium preheated grill for about 3 minutes until just starting to melt.

easy
breakfast
and brunch

easy breakfast basics

AGA toast
Preheat the Aga toaster on the boiling plate for a few minutes (preheating the toaster will prevent the toast from sticking). Toast the bread on each side on the boiling plate with the lid down.

sausages
Sit the grill rack in the Aga roasting tin and arrange the sausages on top. Slide onto the top set of runners in the roasting oven and cook for about 15 minutes, turning halfway through. It's important to sit the sausages on a rack so the fat drains into the base of the tin.

crispy bacon
Arrange the bacon in the Aga roasting tin or arrange it on a baking sheet and slide directly onto the floor of the roasting oven, turn halfway through. Back bacon will take about 8–10 minutes, streaky about 6 minutes.

fried egg
Lift the lid of the simmering plate for a few minutes to let the plate cool down. Cover the lid with a piece of non-stick paper and spread with a little butter. Crack the egg directly onto the buttered area, lower the lid and leave for about 3 minutes, depending on how cooked you like your egg. Sprinkle with salt and pepper and serve. It's possible to fry four eggs on the plate at the same time.

fried mushrooms
Heat a little fat in a roasting tin on the floor of the roasting oven. Toss the mushrooms in the hot fat and return the tin to the floor of the roasting oven for about 8 minutes.

fried tomatoes
Follow the instructions for fried mushrooms.

scrambled eggs and omelettes

Cook in a frying pan on the boiling plate.

kippers

Sit the kippers in an Aga roasting tin. Season and put a knob of butter over each kipper. Cover with foil, slide onto the second set of runners in the roasting oven and cook for about 15–20 minutes.

eggy bread

To make two slices of bread, beat one egg and season with salt and pepper. Spread soft butter thinly on each side of the bread. Heat an Aga roasting tin on the floor of the roasting oven for a few minutes. Dip the bread into the egg and place it in a single layer in the hot roasting tin. Return the tin to the floor of the roasting oven for about 3–4 minutes, turn the bread halfway through until it's crispy and golden brown. These can also be fried in a non-stick frying pan on the simmering plate.

AGA porridge

The best Aga porridge is made overnight in the simmering oven using pinhead oats that unfortunately are only easily available in Scotland. If you don't live north of the border you can use Scots Oats following the instructions below. However, please note that they need to be cooked in the cooler warming oven of the 4 oven Aga and not in the hotter simmering oven.

2- and 3-oven AGAs

Measure quantities according to the packet instructions. Using cold liquid, pour into a saucepan, cover with a lid and sit the pan at the back of the Aga in between the two plates. By the morning the oats will have absorbed the liquid and you will have delicious porridge.

4-oven AGAs

Measure quantities according to packet instructions. Using cold liquid, pour into a saucepan, cover with a lid and transfer to the warming oven overnight (not the simmering oven as it is too hot). By the morning the oats will have absorbed the liquid and you will have delicious porridge.

toasted sandwiches

Assemble your sandwich filling between two slices of bread (not toast). Either grease the simmering plate or cover it with non-stick paper. Sit the sandwich on top, lower the lid and cook for about 3–4 minutes on each side. For an extra special sandwich, butter the outside of the bread; it will be extra crispy, but more fattening!

ideas for fillings
Ham, mango chutney and rocket
Cheese, tomato slices and pesto
Brie and grapes
Pastrami and horseradish
Mozzarella, tomato and basil leaves
Tuna, cheddar and spring onion
Crispy bacon and avocado

toasted open sandwiches
Slice a baguette in half lengthways. Toast the rounded side directly on the boiling plate pressing it down as it toasts. Fill the cut-side with your choice of filling and sit it on non-stick paper on a baking sheet. Slide it onto the top set of runners in the roasting oven. If you have included cheese in your filling, use it to form the top layer and sprinkle with paprika so it turns brown and crispy.

croque monsieur
Toast one side of the bread in the toaster on the boiling plate. Sit the toasted side down onto a baking sheet. Arrange slices of ham on the other side, cover with thin slices of mature Cheddar cheese and sprinkle with a little paprika. Slide onto the top set of runners in the roasting oven for about 5 minutes until the cheese has just melted and is golden brown. Add a fried egg and it becomes, as if by magic, a Croque Madame.

the classic pancake

Here's a basic batter recipe for making pancakes that can be served with lemon and sugar, maple syrup or even banana and ice cream. It can also be used for pancakes with savoury fillings. I cook these directly on the simmering plate but you can, of course, cook them in a frying pan if preferred.

100g (4oz) plain flour
1 egg, beaten
300 ml (½ pint) milk

Measure the flour into a bowl and whisk in the egg and milk until blended. Set aside for about 10 minutes.

Lift the lid of the simmering plate for about 3–5 minutes to cool a little. Using kitchen paper, grease the simmering plate. Spoon half a ladle of batter directly onto the simmering plate, spread out into a circle, using the back of the ladle, about 20cm (8") wide. Cook for 1 minute until bubbles start to appear and, using a palette knife, flip the pancake over and cook for another minute until golden brown. Serve either immediately or leave to cool and then reheat.

To reheat – arrange the pancakes on a plate with greaseproof paper in between the pancakes. Cover in foil and reheat in the simmering oven for about 15 minutes.

makes 6 pancakes

conventional oven
Cook in a frying pan over a high heat.

esgar's eggs

This recipe was invented by my lovely Ma when my three brothers and I were little, and we still love it after all these years.

❄ Not suitable for freezing.

8 eggs
salt and pepper

cheese sauce
25g (1oz) butter
25g (1oz) flour
300ml (½ pint) milk
1 teaspoon Dijon mustard
75g (3oz) mature Cheddar cheese, grated
2 large tomatoes, sliced fairly thinly
little paprika

You will need a shallow ovenproof dish, about 1–1¼ litre (1½–2 pint), buttered.

Put the eggs in a saucepan and cover with water. Bring to the boil on the boiling plate and boil for 10 minutes. Drain and submerge the eggs in cold water. Peel and cut into quarters and arrange them in the base of the dish, season with salt and pepper.

To make the sauce: melt the butter in a pan on the boiling plate, once melted remove from the heat and whisk in the flour and gradually whisk in the milk. Bring to the boil, whisking, add the mustard, salt and pepper and half the cheese. Whisk until bubbling and thickened.

Pour the sauce over the eggs and arrange the tomato slices on top to cover the sauce. Then cover with the remaining cheese and sprinkle with paprika.

Slide the dish onto the top set of runners of the roasting oven for about 12–15 minutes until piping hot.

Serve with some crusty bread.

serves 4

conventional oven
Slide under a preheated grill for about 10–12 minutes until piping hot.

cheesy toad in the hole

I have used cocktail sausages for this recipe but you could use 10 best quality large butcher's sausages.

30 cocktail sausages
4 tablespoons sunflower oil
75g (3oz) mature Cheddar cheese, coarsely grated

batter
100g (4oz) plain flour
3 eggs
225mls (7 floz) milk

Arrange the sausages in a small roasting tin and pour over one tablespoon of the oil. Slide the tin onto the grid shelf on the floor of the roasting oven and roast for about 12–15 minutes until golden brown all over. Remove the sausages using a slotted spoon onto a plate and set aside.

Measure the batter ingredients together and whisk until smooth.

Pour the remaining oil into the tin and slide it onto the floor of the roasting oven and heat for a few minutes. When the oil is piping hot, return the sausages to the pan and immediately pour over the batter mixture and sprinkle the top with cheese. Slide the tin onto the lowest set of runners in the roasting oven for about 25 minutes until well risen and golden brown.

serves 4–6

conventional oven
Cook the sausages in a preheated oven 220C/200C Fan/Gas 7 until golden. Continue as above and bake at the same temperature as the sausages for about 20 minutes until risen and golden.

midday frittata

You could replace the salami in this recipe with ham or bacon, if preferred, or simply for a change.

✳ Not suitable for freezing.

5 eggs
2 tablespoons milk
100g (4oz) salami, snipped into pieces
good knob of butter
100g (4oz) baby spinach
salt and pepper
25g (1oz) sun blushed tomatoes, snipped into quarters
50g (2oz) mature cheddar, grated

Crack the eggs into a bowl and whisk with the milk, season with salt and pepper.

Heat a non-stick frying pan on the boiling plate and fry the salami for a minute until crisp. Add the butter and spinach and fry for a couple of minutes until the spinach starts to wilt, season with salt and pepper. Spread the mixture out so it covers the base of the pan. Pour in the egg mixture and sprinkle over the tomatoes and cheese. Transfer to the simmering plate and continue to fry on the simmering plate for about 3–5 minutes until underneath begins to brown and it starts to set around the edge. Transfer to the top of the roasting oven for about 5 minutes until just set.

Flip over onto a plate or board and serve hot.

serves 4–6

conventional oven
Fry over a high heat on the hob and follow the instructions as above. Slide under a preheated medium grill for about 5 minutes until just set.

easy
pasta and
stir-fries

easy pasta

For all types of pasta, cook in boiling salted water on boiling plate according to packet instructions.

lasagne sheets

If making lasagne and serving immediately I tend to use fresh lasagne sheets, this way the sheets will become tender. If making ahead you can use fresh or dried pasta sheets – the advantage of making ahead is that the sheets soften from the liquid in the sauce and therefore take less time to cook.

easy rice

The best way to cook rice in the Aga is the absorption method. It really is very easy, as long as the quantities of rice to water are correct. Following the chart below: bring to the boil, cover and transfer to the simmering oven.

basmati rice	200g (8oz)	12floz water	15–20 minutes
brown rice	200g (8oz)	14floz water	40–45 minutes
long grain rice	200g (8oz)	12 floz water	20 minutes

If using different quantities to the above, work out the proportions. For example, for Long Grain rice, it's the same amount of water plus half again. Long Grain rice is the same as Easy Cook or American rice.

smoked chicken penne with aubergine and rocket

A brilliantly simple pasta dish – replace the penne for fusilli if you prefer.

❄ Not suitable for freezing.

350g (12oz) penne pasta
5 tablespoons olive oil
1 large aubergine, halved lengthways and thinly sliced
1 large onion, thinly sliced
1 teaspoon sugar
2 cloves garlic, crushed
3 tablespoons balsamic vinegar
250g (9oz) cherry tomatoes, halved
100g (4oz) smoked chicken breast, sliced into thin strips
50g (2oz) fresh rocket leaves, torn in half
50g (2oz) Parmesan cheese, grated

Cook the pasta in boiling salted water, according to packet instructions until just cooked, drain.

Heat 3 tablespoons of the oil in large frying pan on the boiling plate. Add the aubergine, onion and sugar and fry for a few minutes until golden brown.
Add the cooked pasta, the rest of the oil and the remaining ingredients, except the cheese, to the pan and season with salt and pepper. Toss for few minutes on the boiling plate until piping hot.

Serve immediately sprinkled with the Parmesan.

serves 6

conventional oven
Cook on the hob.

spaghetti pomodoro

A classic tomato and basil sauce with the added twist of Mozzarella. For a great variation simply add 150g (5oz) cooked prawns to the sauce at the end.

❄ Not suitable for freezing.

350g (12oz) spaghetti
1 tablespoon oil
1 large onion, finely chopped
2 cloves garlic, crushed
2 x 400g (14oz) tin chopped tomatoes
1 good tablespoon sun-dried tomato paste
1 teaspoon sugar
3 tablespoons fresh basil, chopped
1 x 125g ball Mozzarella, cut into small cubes

Cook the spaghetti in boiling salted water according to packet instructions, drain and set aside.

Heat the oil in a non-stick frying pan. Add the onion and garlic and fry for a few minutes. Add the tomatoes, tomato paste and sugar and boil up for about 4 minutes, stirring. Season with salt and pepper.

Add the cooked spaghetti to the pan and stir to completely coat the spaghetti. Stir in the Mozzarella and basil.

Serve hot.

serves 4–6

conventional oven
Cook on the hob.

pesto and feta fusilli

The punch of the pesto adds to the full-on flavour of one of my favourite pasta dishes. For ease I have recommended you buy a ready-made jar of pesto – the best are very good indeed – but you could, of course, make your own. For this dish I prefer to use basil pesto rather than coriander or rocket.

❄ Not suitable for freezing.

350g (12oz) fusilli pasta
150g (5oz) mange tout, cut in half lengthways
1 tablespoon oil
1 red pepper, thinly sliced
150g (5oz) Feta cheese, cubed
100g (4oz) green olives, halved
4 tablespoons pesto

Cook the pasta in boiling salted water on the boiling plate according to packet instructions. Three minutes before the end of cooking add the mange tout. Drain and rinse with cold water to keep the colour, set aside.

Heat the oil in a non-stick frying pan on the boiling plate. Add the pepper and fry for a minute and then stir in the cheese, olives and pesto. Then add the cooked pasta and mange tout, season and toss the pan on the heat until well mixed and piping hot.

serves 4–6

conventional oven
Cook on the hob.

penne with broccoli, sun-blushed tomato and basil

This is an absolute favourite of mine. Be careful not to overcook the broccoli, it should retain a bit of a crunch once cooked.

❄ Not suitable for freezing.

350g (12oz) penne pasta
225g (8oz) broccoli, cut into tiny florets
150g (5oz) dry cured ham, snipped into pieces
225g (8oz) small chestnut mushrooms, sliced
1 x 200 ml carton full-fat crème fraiche
75g (3oz) sun-blushed tomatoes snipped into pieces
about 50g (2 oz) Parmesan cheese, coarsely grated
2 tablespoons chopped fresh basil

Cook the pasta in a large pan of boiling salted water on the boiling plate, according to packet instructions. Three minutes before the end of cooking add the broccoli florets. Drain and rinse, set aside.

Fry the ham in a large non-stick frying pan on the boiling plate until crisp, remove half of the ham and set aside.

Add the chestnut mushrooms to the frying pan and stir with the ham for a moment, then stir in the crème fraîche, tomatoes and half the Parmesan cheese, season with a little salt and pepper (go easy on the salt as the ham is salty). Bring to the boil and return the cooked pasta and broccoli to the pan. Stir well until piping hot. Check the seasoning.

Sprinkle over the remaining Parmesan, ham and basil. Serve immediately.

serves 4–6

conventional oven
Cook on the hob.

serrano risotto with basil

Risottos are fantastic when cooked in the Aga. Instead of having to stand and stir continuously on the hob, you simply place your rice in the simmering oven and leave to cook to perfection.

❄ Not suitable for freezing.

1 x 70g packet Serrano ham, snipped into small pieces
1 tablespoon oil
1 small red onion, finely chopped
1 red pepper, cut into small dice
225g (8oz) risotto rice
150ml ($1/4$ pint) white wine
600ml (1 pint) chicken stock
salt and pepper
50g (2oz) shavings fresh Parmesan
4 tablespoons fresh basil, torn into pieces

Fry the ham pieces in a non-stick frying pan on the boiling plate until crisp. Remove half and set aside. Add the oil, onion, pepper and rice and fry for a few minutes on the boiling plate. Gradually add the wine and stock and whilst stirring bring to the boil. Season with salt and pepper, cover and transfer to simmering oven for about 15–20 minutes or until the rice is just tender and all the liquid has been absorbed.

Stir in the basil, tip into a serving dish and garnish with shavings of Parmesan.

serves 4–6

conventional oven
Cook over a low heat on the hob.

tarragon chicken tagliatelle with roquefort

I have used tagliatelle here but you could substitute penne or fussilli pasta if preferred. Once cooked this should be served immediately for maximum flavour effect.

❄ Not suitable for freezing.

1 tablespoon oil
3 chicken breast, without skin or bone, cut into very thin strips
salt and pepper
350g (12oz) tagliatelle
225g (8oz) long-stemmed broccoli spears, cut in half lengthways
5 tablespoons double cream
175g (6oz) Roquefort cheese, cut into small cubes
juice of half a lemon
3 tablespoons chopped fresh tarragon

Heat the oil in a deep non-stick frying pan on the boiling plate. Season the chicken strips with salt and pepper and fry until golden brown and cooked through, transfer to a plate.

Cook the pasta in salted boiling water on the boiling plate according to packet instructions. Add the broccoli for the last two minutes until al dente. Drain.

Add the remaining ingredients to the frying pan, stir in the pasta and broccoli and return the chicken to the pan. Stir well, season with salt and pepper.

Serve immediately.

serves 4–6

conventional oven
Cook on the hob.

piquante pork stir-fry

The classic fast-food dish. The use of runny honey gives the pork a lovely golden colour.

❄ Not suitable for freezing.

1 tablespoon oil
350g (12oz) pork fillet, cut into thin strips
1 tablespoon runny honey
8 baby corn, sliced in half lengthways
$\frac{1}{2}$ red pepper, thinly sliced
75g (3oz) mange tout, cut in half lengthways
100g (4oz) pack choi, sliced, white and green parts kept separate
2 tablespoons soy sauce
2 tablespoons sweet chilli dipping sauce
1 tablespoon white wine vinegar
salt and pepper

Heat the oil in a large non-stick frying pan on the boiling plate. Add the pork strips and pour over the honey. Fry for a few minutes until golden brown all over. Remove using a slotted spoon onto a plate and set aside.

Add all the vegetables to the pan, except the green part of the pack choi, and fry on the boiling plate for 3–4 minutes. Return the pork to the pan and add the green parts of the pack choi. Mix together the soy, chilli sauce and vinegar in a small bowl and add 2 tablespoons of water. Pour into the pan and stir-fry for a further 4 minutes or so. Season with salt and pepper.

Serve immediately with boiled rice and prawn crackers.

serves 4

conventional oven
Cook on the hob.

soy salmon and vegetable stir-fry

A beautiful oriental inspired dish full of vibrant colours and subtle flavours.
Cook and then serve immediately.

❄ Not suitable for freezing.

450g (1lb) salmon fillets, middle cut, skinned

marinade
3 tablespoons soy sauce
2 tablespoons runny honey
grated zest and juice of 1 lemon
2cm (1") fresh ginger, peeled and grated

3 tablespoons oil
150g (5oz) mange tout, cut in half lengthways
2 medium carrots, peeled and cut into matchsticks
1 x 200g (7oz) pak choi, thickly sliced
salt and pepper

Slice the salmon fillets lengthways into 8 thin strips. Mix the marinade ingredients together in a large bowl and add the salmon. Toss and leave to marinate for about 30 minutes in the fridge.

Heat a non-stick frying pan on the boiling plate and add 2 tablespoons of the oil, remove the salmon from the marinade and pan-fry for a minute on each side until golden brown. (You may need to fry in batches). Carefully remove with a fish slice onto a plate, cover with foil and keep warm in the simmering oven while stir-frying the vegetables.

Add the remaining oil to the pan, and stir-fry the vegetables on the boiling plate for about 5 minutes. Season with salt and pepper, pour over the reserved marinade and toss until piping hot.

Serve a spoonful of vegetables on each plate with two slices of salmon arranged on top per person.

serves 4

conventional oven
Cook on the hob and keep warm in a low oven.

spiced chicken stir-fry

A spicy and speedy stir-fry incorporating a marinade that makes use of many of your storecupboard standbys. This is a dry marinade, so serve with a little of your best quality soy sauce on the side.

❄ Not suitable for freezing.

4 chicken breasts, skinless, boneless, each cut into four strips

dry marinade
1 teaspoon ground ginger
$\frac{1}{2}$ teaspoon turmeric
$\frac{1}{2}$ teaspoon mild curry powder
2 teaspoons sugar
salt and pepper

2 tablespoons oil
1 small courgette, thinly sliced
$\frac{1}{2}$ cucumber, cut in half lengthways, seeds removed, cut into horseshoe shapes
150g (5oz) mange tout
1 red pepper, thinly sliced

Mix the marinade ingredients together in a bowl and season with salt and pepper. Add the chicken strips to the bowl, toss and leave to marinate for a minimum of about 30 minutes in the fridge.

Heat the oil in large non-stick frying pan on the boiling plate. Stir-fry the chicken strips until golden brown. Add the rest of the ingredients and fry on the boiling plate for a further 3–4 minutes until the vegetables are slightly charred and the chicken is tender.

Serve hot with a drizzle of soy sauce.

serves 4

conventional oven
Cook on the hob.

easy
fish

skate wings with crispy bacon

As skate wings vary in size quite considerably you may need to cook these in batches depending on how they fit into your frying pan.

❄ Not suitable for freezing.

25g (1oz) butter
4 skate wings
225g (8oz) unsmoked bacon lardons
300ml (½ pint) white wine
2 tablespoons double cream
salt and pepper
4 tablespoons chopped fresh parsley

Heat a large non-stick frying pan on the boiling plate and add the butter. Season the skate wings with salt and pepper and fry them on one side for about 2 minutes until golden brown. Transfer them to a large roasting tin, brown side up. Slide the tin onto the grid shelf on the floor of the roasting oven for about 10 minutes until the fish is cooked through.

While the skate is roasting, make the sauce. Place the same pan on the boiling plate and fry the bacon till crisp. Pour in the wine and reduce by half, stir in the cream, season with salt and pepper and add the parsley at the last minute.

Pour the sauce over the wings and serve.

serves 4

conventional oven
Cook in a pan on the hob.

sole goujons with mustard and chive dip

This recipe couldn't be easier. The use of mustard is very subtle but it you are not a great lover of Dijon's finest then simply brush with beaten egg instead. Serve as a main course or as a starter.

❋ Freezes well raw and coated.

3 large lemon sole fillets, skinned and each one sliced into 6 long thin strips
3 tablespoons grainy mustard
50g (2oz) white breadcrumbs
2 tablespoons fresh chives, snipped
1 tablespoon oil

mustard and chive dip
2 tablespoons grainy mustard
1 x 200ml carton half-fat crème fraîche
2 tablespoons fresh chives, snipped
juice $\frac{1}{2}$ lemon
1 teaspoon sugar
salt and pepper

Put the sole goujons into a mixing bowl, season with salt and pepper and add the mustard. Using your hands, mix until all the goujons have become coated in mustard. Mix the breadcrumbs and chives together on a plate. Dip each goujon into the breadcrumbs to coat each side.

Heat the oil in a frying pan on the boiling plate and fry for about a minute on each side until cooked through.

Mix all the dip ingredients together and season with salt and pepper. Serve the hot goujons with the dip.

serves 4

conventional oven
Pan-fry the breaded goujons in a frying pan on the hob.

mounts bay lasagne

This is my easy version of lasagne, making use of a very simple and quick-to-make sauce – delicious none the less. If you want to use dried lasagne sheets instead of fresh, then soak them first in hot water for about 10 minutes to soften.

❄ Not suitable for freezing.

tomato sauce
1 tablespoon oil
1 onion, finely chopped
2 cloves garlic, crushed
2 x 400g (14oz) tins chopped tomatoes
2 teaspoons sugar
juice and zest of 1 small lemon
salt and pepper
2 tablespoons fresh basil, chopped

450g (1lb) cod, skinned, cut into large cubes
100g (4oz) cooked mussels, without shells
250g (9oz) North Atlantic cooked prawns
150 ml ($\frac{1}{4}$ pint) double cream
6 sheets fresh lasagne, softened for 5 minutes in boiling water
100g (4oz) mature Cheddar, grated

You will need a 3 litre (5 pint) shallow ovenproof dish, buttered.

Heat the oil in a large frying pan on the boiling plate and add the onion, fry for a couple of minutes. Cover and transfer to the simmering oven for about 15 minutes. Return the pan to the boiling plate and add the remaining sauce ingredients, season with salt and pepper and simmer on the simmering plate for about 5 minutes, stir in the basil.

Spoon out one third of the sauce into a bowl and mix with the cod, mussels and prawns. Season with salt and pepper.

Spoon half the remaining tomato sauce into the base of your buttered dish, pour a third of the cream and a third of the cheddar on top. Arrange 3 sheets of lasagne on top, spoon over the tomato-coated seafood. Pour over half the remaining double cream and the Cheddar, top with 3 sheets of lasagne and finish with tomato sauce, cream and the remaining Cheddar.

Slide onto the second set of runners of the roasting oven for about 20–25 minutes until the fish is cooked, golden brown and bubbling around the edge.

serves 6

conventional oven
Bake in a pre-heated oven 180C/160C Fan/Gas 4 for 20–25 minutes.

pesto cod with basil

You could substitute the cod for sea bass or bream. But whichever fish you use be very careful not to overcook the fillets.

❋ Not suitable for freezing.

4 x 150g (5oz) cod fillets, skinned

topping
2 tablespoons full-fat crème fraîche
2 tablespoons green pesto
grated zest of 1 lemon
2 tablespoons chopped fresh basil
salt and pepper

Arrange the cod fillets on a baking sheet and season with salt and pepper.

Mix the topping ingredients together in a bowl, season with salt and pepper. Spread the mixture on top of each cod fillet.

Slide the baking sheet onto the grid shelf on the floor of the roasting oven for about 8–10 minutes until the cod is just cooked.

Serve hot with a squeeze of lemon.

serves 4

conventional oven
Bake in a pre-heated oven 190C/170C Fan/Gas 5 for about 10 minutes.

fresh sardines with warm tomato dressing

Though you could cook the sardines in a frying pan on the boiling plate, I find it easier, and also less messy, to cook them on the floor of the roasting oven. Strictly speaking the skins should be removed from the tomatoes, but life's just too short for that!

❄ Not suitable for freezing.

4 x large sardines, head on, gutted and de-scaled
olive oil, for coating the fish

tomato dressing
2 tablespoons olive oil
1 shallot, finely chopped
3 tomatoes, seeds removed and roughly chopped
3 tablespoons flat leaf parsley, chopped
juice of 1 lemon
salt and pepper

Rub each fish with a little oil and season with salt and pepper. Arrange on a baking sheet. Slide directly onto the floor of the roasting oven and bake the fish for about 3 minutes on each side, turning halfway through.

Measure the olive oil into a frying pan. Add the shallot and fry on the boiling plate for about 4 minutes until golden. Add the remaining ingredients and fry for a minute, season with salt and pepper.

Arrange the sardines on a serving platter and pour the warm dressing over the tail half of the fish.

serves 4

conventional oven
Cook the sardines under a low grill for about 3 minutes on each side.

seafood green curry with papaya

My lovely friend Sousie who lives in Perth, Australia gave me inspiration for this recipe. It's fairly mild so if you like your curries on the hotter side you could always add a little more green Thai curry paste at the end of cooking.

❄ Not suitable for freezing.

1 tablespoon oil
1 small green chilli, seeds removed, finely chopped
2cm (1") fresh ginger, finely grated
1 clove garlic, crushed
finely grated zest and juice of 1 lime
1 x 400g (14oz) can coconut milk
1 tablespoon green Thai curry paste
$\frac{1}{2}$ teaspoon fish sauce
450g (1lb) fresh cod, cut into 2cm (1") chunks
175g (6oz) fresh prawns, cooked
salt and pepper
$\frac{1}{4}$ just ripe papaya, peeled, cut into thin strips
2 tablespoons fresh basil, chopped

Heat the oil in a non-stick frying pan on the boiling plate. Add the chilli, ginger, garlic and lime zest and fry for a minute.

Pour in the coconut milk and stir. Add the curry paste, fish sauce, cod and prawns, season with a little salt and pepper. Stirring, continue to cook on the boiling plate for about 5 minutes until the cod is just cooked.

Add the lime juice, papaya and basil and heat through. Serve immediately with rice.

serves 6

conventional oven
Cook on the hob.

salmon and watercress quiche

A wonderfully fresh tasting quiche that is so simple to make because there is no pre-baking of the pastry case.

❄ Not suitable for freezing.

pastry
225g (8oz) flour
100g (4oz) butter
1 egg, beaten
1–2 tablespoons water

filling
5 eggs
300ml (½ pint) double cream
150ml (¼ pint) milk
salt and pepper
350g (12oz) salmon fillet, skinned and sliced into long very thin strips
50g (2oz) watercress, very roughly chopped
75g (3oz) mature Cheddar cheese, grated
3 tablespoons fresh dill, chopped

Measure the flour and butter into a processor and whiz until like breadcrumbs. Add the egg and water and whiz again till a dough ball forms. Wrap the dough in clingfilm and rest in the fridge.

Whisk the eggs, cream and milk together in a bowl, season with salt and pepper.

Roll the pastry out and line a 28cm (11") loose-bottomed flan tin. Scatter the raw slices of salmon and watercress over the base of the pastry. Sprinkle over dill and cheese and season with salt and pepper. Pour over the egg mixture.

Slide onto the floor of the roasting oven for about 30 minutes until golden brown on top and the filling is set and the pastry is crisp. If it's getting too brown, slide the cold sheet onto the second set of runners.

Serve warm with a dressed salad.

serves 6–8

conventional oven
Bake the pastry blind in a preheated oven 180C/160C Fan/Gas 4 for about 15 minutes. Fill the case with the mixture and return it to the oven at the same temperature for about 25 minutes until golden brown and the filling is set.

sesame lemon sole with pak choi stir-fry

A really clever way to treat sole, this Chinese inspired dish was invented by my brilliant assistant Lucinda.

❄ Not suitable for freezing.

3 tablespoons oil
4 large lemon sole fillets, skinned

stir-fry
2 cloves garlic, crushed
175g (6oz) shitake mushrooms, thinly sliced
350g (12oz) pak choi, sliced thickly lengthways
3 tablespoons hoi sin sauce
3 tablespoons soy sauce
salt and pepper
2 tablespoons sesame seeds

Heat 2 tablespoons of the oil in a large non-stick frying pan on the boiling plate. Season the sole fillets and fry them for about 1$\frac{1}{2}$ minutes on each side. Transfer to a plate, cover with foil and keep them warm in the simmering oven whilst cooking the stir-fry.

Heat the remaining oil in a wok on the boiling plate and stir-fry the remaining ingredients for a few minutes, stirring all the time. Season with salt and pepper and sprinkle half the sesame seeds over.

Divide the stir-fry between four plates and place a hot sole fillet on top, pour over the sauce and sprinkle with the remaining sesame seeds.

Serve immediately.

serves 4

conventional oven
Cook over a high heat on the hob.

simple tuna fishcakes

So quick to make, no precooking to do, just mix and shape. If preferred, you can cook the fishcakes in a frying pan on the boiling plate in a little oil for 4–5 minutes on each side rather than in the roasting oven.

❋ Not suitable for freezing.

3 thick slices brown bread
5 tablespoons mayonnaise
2 x 130g tins tuna, in oil, drained and dried
50g (2oz) mature Cheddar cheese, grated
8 Peppadew peppers, coarsely sliced
2 tablespoons fresh parsley, coarsely chopped
salt and pepper

Break the bread into a processor and whiz until you have fine breadcrumbs. Tip a third of the breadcrumbs onto a plate and set aside. Add the remaining ingredients to the breadcrumbs in the processor and season with salt and pepper. Whiz until just combined but still with a texture.

Shape the mixture into 6 large or 8 small cakes about 2cm (1") thick. Dip them into the breadcrumbs until coated all over. Arrange on a baking sheet and drizzle over a tiny bit of oil.

Slide onto the floor of the roasting oven for about 5 minutes on each side, carefully turning over half way through, until crisp and golden brown.

Serve piping hot with a dressed green salad.

serves 6

conventional oven
Fry in a little oil in a frying pan over high heat for about 5 minutes on each side.

the king of the sea

For me, Dover sole is the king of the sea. I think this is the best way to treat this wonderful fish. The secret to success is to fry the sole briefly on the boiling plate of the Aga and to then transfer it to the oven to finish cooking.

❄ Not suitable for freezing.

2 Dover soles, skinned both sides, head on
salt and pepper
good knob of butter

Heat a large frying pan on the boiling plate. Season the soles with salt and pepper on both sides.

Add the butter to the hot pan and fry each fish on one side for about 2 minutes until golden brown. Transfer to a large roasting tin with the brown side uppermost. Transfer to the grid shelf on the floor of the roasting oven for about 8–10 minutes until cooked through.

Serve hot with a squeeze of lemon.

serves 2

conventional oven
Fry over a high heat on one side for about 4 minutes, turn over and continue to cook on the other side for further 4 minutes until cooked through.

thai salmon with avocado and lime

This perfect dinner party dish is a total winner every time! It's really speedy to make and has beautifully subtle Thai flavours.

❄ Not suitable for freezing.

4 x 150g (5oz) middle-cut salmon fillets, skinned
salt and pepper

avocado filling
2 small ripe avocados, peeled
zest and juice of 1 lime
1 teaspoon Thai curry paste

sauce
1 tablespoon soy sauce
2 tablespoons sweet chilli dipping sauce
2 tablespoons water

lime slices to garnish
sprigs of flat leaf parsley to garnish

Slice the salmon fillets in half horizontally so you have 8 thin fillets, season with salt and pepper.

To make the filling: mash all the filling ingredients together until nearly smooth but still with a little texture. Divide the filling mixture into four portions and spread one portion each onto the tops of four of the halved fillets. Sit the remaining fillets on top of the filling to make a complete fillet again. Sit them on a greased baking sheet or roasting tin.

Slide the tin onto the grid shelf on the floor of the roasting oven for about 8–10 minutes until the salmon is just cooked.

For the sauce: measure the ingredients into a saucepan and heat on the simmering plate until hot. Serve the salmon with a little sauce and garnish with lime slices and a sprig of flat leaf parsley.

serves 4

conventional oven
Bake in preheated oven 180C/160C Fan/Gas 4 for about 10 minutes until the salmon is cooked through.

easy
meat,
poultry and game

the AGA roast

roast chicken

To prepare the chicken: season all over and spread the breast with soft butter. Fill the cavity of the chicken with some flavourings of your choice such as lemon, onion wedges and herbs. Stand the chicken on the grill rack in a roasting tin and cover the breasts with foil. Slide onto the lowest set of runners in the roasting oven.

900g (2lb) chicken	about 45 minutes
1.5kg (3lb) chicken	about 1 hour
1.75kg (4lb) chicken	about $1\frac{1}{2}$ hours

Remove the foil towards the end of roasting to brown the breast. To test that the chicken is cooked, insert a skewer into the thickest part of the thigh, if the juices run clear the chicken is cooked.

roast pheasant

To prepare the pheasant: season all over and cover the breasts with streaky bacon. Sit the bird in the roasting tin. Slide it onto the second set of runners in the roasting oven and roast for about 45–50 minutes until golden brown. To test if the pheasant is cooked insert a skewer into the thickest part of the thigh: if the juices run clear the pheasant is cooked.

roast duck

To prepare the duck: season all over, prick the skin and sit it upside-down on a grill rack in the roasting tin. Slide the tin onto the lowest set of runners in the roasting oven for about 20 minutes. Turn the duck over and roast in the same position for a further 15 minutes or until the duck skin is brown and crispy. Transfer to the simmering oven for about an hour to continue cooking. Return it to roasting oven for about 10 minutes to re-crisp the skin. To test if the duck is cooked insert a skewer into the thickest part of the thigh: if the juices run clear the duck is cooked.

roast goose

For a 4.5–5kg (10–12lb) goose. To prepare the goose: season all over, prick the skin and sit it upside-down on a grill rack in the roasting tin. Slide it onto the lowest set of runners in the roasting oven for about 30 minutes. Turn the goose over and roast in the same position for a further 20 minutes or until the skin is brown and crispy. Transfer to the simmering oven for about 2 hours to continue cooking. Return to the roasting oven for about 10 minutes to re-crisp the skin. To test if the goose is cooked insert a skewer into the thickest part of the thigh: if the juices run clear the goose is cooked.

roast turkey

Prepare the turkey for the oven. Season all over and spread soft butter over the breast. Fill the cavity of the turkey with flavourings such as lemon, onion wedges and herbs. Line the roasting tin with foil. Stand the turkey on the grill rack in the roasting tin and sit the turkey on the rack and cover the breasts with foil.

slow roasting

3.6–4.5kg (8–10lb)	about 8–10 hours
5–7.25kg (11–16lb)	about 9–12 hours
7.5–10kg (17–22lb)	about 10–14 hours

Slide directly into the simmering oven and follow the timings above. For the last 30 minutes, remove the foil and transfer the turkey to the roasting oven to brown the skin. Test that the turkey is cooked by inserting a skewer into the thickest part of the thigh, if the juices run clear the turkey is cooked.

fast roasting
Prepare the turkey as above. Slide onto the lowest set of runners in the roasting oven.

3.6–4.5kg (8–10lb)	about $1^3/_4$–2 hours
5–7.25kg (11–16lb)	about $2^1/_2$ hours
7.5–10kg (17–22lb)	about 3 hours

For the last 30 minutes, remove the foil and transfer to the roasting oven to brown the skin. Test for doneness as above. Leave to rest (see p82).

roast beef

topside, sirloin and prime rib
These times are for a pink medium-rare centre. Roasting oven:

On the bone	12 minutes per 450g (1lb)
Off the bone	15 minutes per 450g (lb)

If you like it well done add about 5 minutes per 450g (1lb).

fillet
Firstly brown the steak in a frying pan to seal the meat, transfer to a roasting tin and slide it onto the top set of runners of the roasting oven.

Browned fillet takes about 10 minutes per 450g (1lb).

brisket and silverside
As these are tougher cuts of meat I would suggest starting in the roasting oven to brown and then transfer covered to the simmering oven.

Cook as a pot roast for about 1 hour per 450g (1lb) basting regularly.

roast pork

To get perfect crackling, score the skin well, rub with oil and cover with sea salt. If the joint is very large and the skin runs under the meat, using a sharp knife remove the skin and roast it separately. Do not keep the crackling warm, as it will become soggy.

boned loin pork

Roasting oven.

> About 25 minutes per 450g (1lb).

roast lamb

Prepare for the oven, and season well. I like to sit my roast on sprigs of rosemary before roasting. Roasting oven:

leg and shoulder

| Pink | 15 minutes per 450g (1lb) |
| Well done | 20 minutes per 450g (1lb) |

saddle

> About 45 minutes per 3kg (6$\frac{1}{2}$lb) saddle.

rack of lamb

Based on two racks (about 7 chops in each).

> About 15–20 minutes for Pink.

lamb loin fillet

Based on 2 lamb loins (about 550g/1lb 4oz). Seal in a frying pan on boiling plate first.

> About 8–12 minutes for Pink.

important: resting your roast

For all roasts it is important to rest the meat before carving, this sets the juices preventing the meat from drying out and also makes carving easier. Wrap the joint in foil and rest out of the oven, or rest in the simmering oven but remember if you leave it in the oven it will carry on cooking so slightly under roast before transferring.

stocks

The Aga is perfect for making stock, no hassle as the ovens are ready and waiting. Here are a few stock tips:

- Never mix raw bones and cooked bones.
- Add flavourings – such as onion, celery, carrots, parsley stalks and bay leaf.
- Don't use green vegetables as they make the stock slimy.
- Don't use starchy vegetables such as potatoes as they make the stock cloudy, nor strongly flavoured root vegetables such as celeriac and parsnip.
- For beef stock ask the butcher to saw large bones into manageable pieces so they will fit easily into a saucepan.
- For large bones such as a chicken carcass, freeze in large poly bags and bash with a wooden rolling pin and they will break up easily.
- Measure stock into empty cream or yoghurt pots and then freeze. This will help when making a recipe – the stock is already measured for you.
- Always sieve a stock just in case there are small splinters of bone.
- Season with salt and pepper, but don't overdo it, bearing in mind you will be seasoning the dish as well.
- For a really intensely flavoured stock reduce until it is very dark brown.

poultry or game stock

Pack bones tightly in a saucepan and add vegetables such as carrots and onions cut into chunks. Just cover with water and bring to the boil, cover and transfer to simmering oven for about 2 hours until golden brown. Sieve and store in plastic pots.

beef stock

Firstly, brown the beef bones on the floor of the roasting oven, this gives a deeper flavour and brown colour to the stock. Pack them tightly in a saucepan, add vegetables, just cover with water and bring to the boil, cover and transfer to the simmering oven for about 4 hours. Sieve and store in plastic pots.

vegetable stock

Cut vegetables into chunks eg carrots, onions, celery, spring onions whites, bayleaf, peppercorns, parsley stalks, onion skins. Pack them tightly in a saucepan and just cover with water. Bring to the boil, cover and transfer to the simmering oven for about 1–2 hours until well flavoured. Sieve and store in plastic cartons.

pesto chicken with garlic mushrooms and spinach

Moist chicken breasts sitting on a bed of garlicky mushrooms, spinach and pepper – all cooked at once for maximum ease and flavour. Serve with potatoes or rice.

❄ Not suitable for freezing.

2 tablespoons oil
450g (1lb) mixed mushrooms e.g. oyster, shitake, chestnut, very coarsely sliced
2 large garlic cloves, crushed
225g (8oz) fresh baby spinach, stalks removed
$1/2$ teaspoon grated nutmeg
4 tablespoons full-fat crème fraîche
1 tablespoon green pesto
4 chicken breasts, boneless, skinned
2 tablespoons green pesto
salt and pepper
1 x 350g jar roasted red peppers without skin, sliced into long thin strips

Heat the oil in a large non-stick frying pan on the boiling plate. Add the mushrooms and garlic and fry for 1 minute. Add the spinach and nutmeg and continue to fry, stirring for a minute until just wilted. Stir in the crème fraîche and the tablespoon of pesto and season with salt and pepper.

Spread the top of each chicken breast with half a teaspoon of pesto and sprinkle with salt and pepper. Arrange a few slices of pepper randomly on top of each chicken breast, so the top is covered. Stir the remaining pepper strips into the mushroom mixture.

Tip the mushroom mixture into the base of an ovenproof dish, sitting the chicken breasts in a single layer on top. Slide the dish onto the grid shelf on the floor of the roasting oven for about 30 – 35 minutes until the chicken is tender.

Serve piping hot.

serves 4

conventional oven
Bake in a preheated oven 200C/180C Fan/Gas 6 for about 25 minutes until the chicken is tender.

chicken breasts with mushrooms and white wine sauce

This is a classic recipe with the twist of the addition of fennel. Can be made up to 24 hours ahead.

❄ Freezes well.

2 tablespoons oil
4 chicken breasts, boneless, without skin
1 large bulb fennel, thinly sliced
100g (4oz) chestnut mushrooms, thinly sliced
300 ml ($\frac{1}{2}$ pint) white wine
150 ml ($\frac{1}{4}$ pint) double cream
salt and pepper
2 tablespoons fresh parsley, chopped

Heat 1 tablespoon of oil in a large non-stick frying pan on the boiling plate. Season the chicken breasts with salt and pepper and fry on both sides until golden brown. Transfer to an oven-proof dish so they fit snugly in a single layer.

Heat the remaining oil in the same pan, add the fennel and mushrooms and fry on the boiling plate for a couple of minutes. Add the wine and reduce by half, add the cream and reduce again until the sauce thickens. Season with salt and pepper. Pour over the chicken breasts in the dish.

Cover with foil, slide onto the grid shelf on the floor of the roasting oven for about 30–35 minutes until the chicken is tender.

Serve hot sprinkled with parsley.

serves 4

conventional oven
Bake in a preheated oven 180C/160C Fan/Gas 4 for about 30 minutes until the chicken is tender.

chicken el socorrat

Beautifully browned and succulent chicken thighs in a ratatouille-style Provencal sauce with the addition of a dash of southern Spain in the shape of chorizo. You could use chicken breasts instead of thighs but remember that they will take a shorter time to cook.

❄ Not suitable for freezing.

1 tablespoon oil
6 chicken thighs, bone in, skin removed
2 tablespoons paprika
100g (4oz) chorizo, cut into pieces, the size of a hazelnut
1 red pepper, cut into large wedges
2 medium courgettes, cut into cubes
1 onion, sliced
3 cloves garlic, crushed
2 x 400g (14oz) tins chopped tomatoes
1 tablespoon mango chutney
2 tablespoons of balsamic vinegar
1 large bunch of basil, chopped

Heat the oil in a deep saucepan or casserole dish on the boiling plate. Sprinkle the thighs with paprika and salt and pepper. Brown on both sides until golden brown, remove and set aside.

Add the chorizo, pepper, courgette, onion and garlic to the pan and fry on the boiling plate for a few minutes. Stir in the chopped tomatoes and return the chicken to the pan. Bring to the boil, cover and transfer to the simmering oven for about 45 minutes until the chicken is tender and vegetables are soft.

Stir in the balsamic vinegar and mango chutney and sprinkle in the basil. Serve hot with rice or mash.

serves 6

conventional oven
Fry over a high heat to brown the chicken. Continue as above and bring to the boil, cover and simmer over a low heat for about 50 minutes until the chicken is tender.

escalope of chicken with dijon sauce

Simple, classic and delicious – which is exactly why it is a classic!

❄ Not suitable for freezing.

4 chicken breasts, boneless and skinless
1 teaspoon paprika
1 teaspoon of ground ginger
1 tablespoon oil
1 x 200ml carton half-fat crème fraîche
1 tablespoon Dijon mustard
salt and pepper

Lay each chicken breast between two pieces of clingfilm and beat using a mallet or the base of a saucepan bash until it's half as thick.

Sprinkle the chicken with salt, pepper, paprika and ginger on both sides.
Heat the oil in wide-based non-stick frying pan on the boiling plate. Fry the chicken for 3–4 minutes on each side until golden brown and cooked in the middle.

Mix the crème fraîche and mustard together, season with salt and pepper. Pour into the frying pan with the chicken and allow it to boil for a couple of minutes.

Serve the chicken piping hot with the sauce poured over the top.

serves 4

conventional oven
Cook over a high heat on the hob.

taverna chicken

The sauce is cooked together with the chicken in this Greek inspired dish, so no last minute panic.

❄ Not suitable for freezing

6 chicken breasts, boneless and skinless

filling
75g (3oz) Feta cheese, cut into small cubes
salt and pepper
1 tablespoon sun-dried tomato paste
25g (1oz) black olives, coarsely chopped
1 tablespoon fresh basil leaves, chopped

sauce
1 x 500g carton passata
juice $\frac{1}{2}$ a lemon
1 tablespoon soy sauce
1 tablespoon runny honey

Grease a 2.4 litre (4 pint) shallow ovenproof dish or small roasting tin.

Season the chicken breasts with salt and pepper and lay them on a board. Using a sharp knife slit them lengthways along the top of the chicken, two thirds of the way through.

Mix together all the filling ingredients in a bowl, mashing the Feta with a fork, and season with salt and pepper. Using your hand, press the filling into the slit in the chicken. Mix the sauce ingredients and pour into the prepared dish. Arrange the chicken breasts snugly on top of the sauce.

Slide the dish onto the second set of runners of the roasting oven for about 30–35 minutes or until the chicken is tender and piping hot.

serves 6

conventional oven
Bake in a preheated oven 180C/160C Fan/Gas 4 for about 30–35 minutes until tender.

boxing day pie

The salvation for left over turkey at Christmas. You could also use left over chicken and enjoy this brilliant pie all the year round.

❄ Freezes well without the potato topping.

40g (1½oz) butter
1 large onion, finely chopped
40g (1½oz) flour
150 ml (¼ pint) white wine
450ml (¾ pint) milk
1 tablespoon grainy mustard
250g (9oz) chestnut or closed cup mushrooms, thickly sliced
2 tablespoons fresh parsley, chopped
450g (1lb) turkey, cooked and shredded into thick strips
salt and pepper
900g (2lb) potatoes, peeled, cut into cubes
milk and butter for mashing
75g (3oz) Cheddar cheese, grated

Butter a 2.2 litre (3½ pint) shallow ovenproof dish.

Heat the butter in a non-stick pan on the boiling plate. Add the onion and fry for a minute. Whisk in the flour and blend in the wine and milk, whisking continuously until smooth and bubbling. Stir in the mustard, mushrooms, parsley and turkey. Season with salt and pepper. Tip the sauce into the dish and set aside to cool.

Boil the potatoes in salted water on the boiling plate until tender (this will depend on the size you have cut them up). Drain and mash with a little milk and butter. Season with salt and pepper and then spoon the mash on top of the cooled turkey mixture. Spread over evenly and sprinkle with cheese.

Slide the dish onto the second set of runners in the roasting oven for about 25–30 minutes until golden brown and bubbling around the edges.

serves 6

conventional oven
Cook the pie in a preheated oven 200C/180C Fan/Gas 6 for about 30–35 minutes.

oriental chicken burgers

The quickest burgers you will ever make. Delicious when served either with salad or in a bun. You can fry them all on the boiling plate but I like to cook them half on top and half in the roasting oven which is easier than frying them in batches.

❄ They freeze well raw.

4 chicken breasts, boneless, skinned
1 small carrot, peeled and grated
4 spring onions, finely sliced white and green
4 tablespoons Hoisin sauce
salt and pepper
1 egg, beaten
2 tablespoons sunflower oil

Cut the chicken breasts into quarters and whiz them in a processor until finely chopped. Tip into a large mixing bowl.

Add the rest of the ingredients to the bowl, except the egg. Mix together with your hands until evenly spread. Gradually add a little egg to the mixture until the mixture has become combined but not wet (you may not need all the egg).

Put a little oil on your hands and shape the mixture into 12 thin even-sized burgers and chill for at least 10 minutes to firm them up.

Heat 1 tablespoon of oil in a non-stick frying pan on the boiling plate and brown the burgers for a couple of minutes on one side, transfer to a greased baking sheet with the browned side up.

Slide the sheet onto the floor of the roasting oven for about 7–10 minutes until the burgers are golden brown and cooked through.

makes 12 burgers

conventional oven
Fry over a high heat for about 4 minutes on each side.

ruda chicken broth

A chicken and vegetable soup that has the unusual and delicious addition of mashed potato. Very hearty and warming and a meal in itself.

❄ Not suitable for freezing.

1 onion, finely sliced
2 large carrots, thinly sliced on the diagonal
salt and pepper
2.1 litres (3½ pints) of chicken stock
750g (1½ lb) potatoes
2 tablespoons milk
3 tablespoons fresh parsley, chopped
350g (12oz) chicken, cooked and shredded into thin strips

Put the onion, carrot and stock into a deep saucepan, bring to the boil on the boiling plate. Cover and transfer to the simmering oven for about 30 minutes until the vegetables are tender. Season with salt and pepper.

Meanwhile, cut the potatoes into cubes and boil them in salted water until tender. Mash with the milk and season with salt and pepper.

Add the shredded chicken to the hot soup and bring to the boil to heat through.

Spoon a volcano shape of mashed potato in the centre of 6 soup bowls. Spoon the hot soup over and sprinkle with parsley.

serves 6

conventional oven
Simmer over a low heat for about 25 minutes until the vegetables are tender.

burghley pheasant

A simple pheasant breast casserole cooked in a rich and slightly sweet parsnip and Madeira sauce.

❄ Freezes well cooked.

1 tablespoon oil
6 pheasant breasts, skinned
25g (1oz) butter
1 leek, sliced
1 large parsnip, peeled and cut into 1cm (½") cubes
25g (1oz) flour
50 ml (2floz) Madeira
250 ml (8floz) pheasant or chicken stock
salt and pepper

Heat the oil in a deep non-stick frying pan or casserole on the boiling plate. Season the breasts with salt and pepper and fry till golden brown on each side. Remove and set aside.

Add the butter to the same pan and fry the leeks and parsnips for a couple of minutes. Remove from the heat, sprinkle in the flour and return the pan to the boiling plate, gradually add the Madeira and stock, stirring all the time. Return the pheasant to the pan and bring to the boil. Season with salt and pepper, cover and transfer to the simmering oven for about 35–45 minutes till the pheasant and parsnips are tender.

Serve hot with creamy mash.

serves 6

conventional oven
Cook on the hob as above. Bring to the boil, transfer to a preheated oven 180C/ 160C Fan/Gas 4 for about 30–40 minutes until the pheasant and parsnips are tender.

duck breasts with oyster mushrooms and red wine sauce

The sauce can be made ahead and the duck breasts reheated from cold in the roasting oven for about 12 minutes just prior to serving.

❊ Not suitable for freezing.

2 tablespoons oil
6 duck breasts, skin removed
salt and pepper
450g (1llb) oyster mushrooms, cut in quarters
200 ml (7 floz) red wine
200 ml (7floz) good game stock
1 teaspoon of tomato purée
1 teaspoon of balsamic vinegar
knob of butter

Heat 1 tablespoon of the oil in frying pan on the boiling plate. Season the duck breasts with salt and pepper. Fry the duck for about 3 minutes on each side until golden brown, transfer to the roasting tin and roast on the top set of runners in the roasting oven for about 7 minutes until tender but still pink.

To make the sauce: using the same unwashed frying pan on the boiling plate, heat the remaining tablespoon of oil. Add the mushrooms and fry for couple of minutes. Add the red wine, stock and tomato purée and reduce until nearly half the amount. Season with salt and pepper, add balsamic vinegar and whisk in the butter just before serving.

Carve the duck breasts in three on the diagonal and serve with spoonful of mushroom sauce.

serves 6

conventional oven
Fry the duck breasts over a high heat on the hob. Transfer to a roasting tin and roast in a preheated oven 200C/180C Fan/Gas 6 for about 8 minutes until tender but still pink in the middle. Continue making the sauce on the hob as above.

braised mulled wine beef

The Aga is the perfect cooker for braised dishes. The delicious sauce is made from the juices and vegetables. The beef should be well done and tender when cooked.

❄ Not suitable for freezing.

3 tablespoons sunflower oil
1.5kg (3lb) topside beef joint
2 small leeks, sliced
2 small carrots, roughly chopped
350g (12oz) swede, peeled and cut into small cubes
600ml (1 pint) red wine
1 teaspoon mixed spice powder
600ml (1 pint) beef stock
2 tablespoons of tomato purée
salt and pepper
1 large sprig fresh thyme
2 tablespoons apricot jam

Heat 1 tablespoon of the oil in large casserole dish. Brown the beef for a few minutes on each side and set aside.

Add the remaining oil to the pan and fry the vegetables for about 3–4 minutes. Sprinkle over the spice and add the wine and stock and bring to the boil, stirring. Stir in the tomato purée, season and add the sprig of thyme. Return the beef to the pan, bring to the boil, cover with a lid and transfer to the simmering oven for about 2–2$\frac{1}{2}$ hours, turning the beef every 40 minutes or so, until it is tender.

Remove the meat from the pan, cover with foil and keep warm in the simmering oven. Remove the thyme stalk and discard. Pour the vegetables and sauce into a processor and whiz until smooth. Return them to the pan, add the apricot jam and check the seasoning.

Carve the hot beef and serve with the hot sauce and mash.

serves 6

conventional oven
Brown the beef on the hob. Cover and cook in a preheated oven 165C/145C Fan/ Gas 3 for about 2 hours until the beef is tender.

lemon spiced beef

A hearty, warming stew, full of flavour, and perfect served with mustard flavoured mash.

❄ Freezes well.

1–2 tablespoons oil
750g (1$\frac{1}{2}$lb) braising steak, cut into 2cm (1") cubes
1 large onion, thinly sliced
2 cloves garlic, crushed
1 medium aubergine, cut into 2cm (1") cubes
1 tablespoon paprika powder
150 ml ($\frac{1}{4}$ pint) red wine
1 x 225g (8oz) tin chopped tomatoes
salt and pepper
1 small lemon
2 tablespoons mango chutney

Heat 1 tablespoon of the oil in a large non-stick frying pan or casserole dish on the boiling plate. Add the beef and brown on all sides (you may need to do this in batches) using a slotted spoon transfer to a plate and set aside.

Add a little more oil if needed and then add the onion, garlic, and aubergine, fry for a minute or two. Sprinkle in the paprika, fry for another minute, stirring continuously. Blend in the wine and tomatoes, season with salt and pepper. Return the beef to the pan and add the lemon whole. Bring to the boil, cover and transfer to the simmering oven for about 1$\frac{1}{2}$–2 hours until the meat is tender.

Once the beef is tender and the lemon soft, pierce and squeeze out about 1 good tablespoon of juice from the lemon, discard the rest. Stir in the chutney and serve piping hot.

serves 6

conventional oven
Cover and cook in a preheated oven 165C/140C Fan/Gas 3 for about 2 hours until tender.

malay beef

I adore this recipe. A brilliantly simple marinade, 1 minute or so of stir-frying and voila! A dish that is guaranteed to become a firm favourite.

❄ Not suitable for freezing.

marinade
2 tablespoons tomato ketchup
2 tablespoons mango chutney
1 tablespoon soy sauce
4cm (2") fresh ginger, peeled and finely grated
a few drops Tabasco
1 tablespoon oil
salt and pepper

500g (1lb) sirloin beef joint

Mix together all the marinade ingredients in a bowl, season with salt and pepper.

Slice the beef into very thin long slices, about $\frac{1}{2}$cm in thickness. Add the slices of beef to the marinade and toss to coat, leave to marinate in the fridge for a couple of hours.

Heat a non-stick frying pan on the boiling plate. Fry the beef for about 30 seconds on each side so it's just pink in the middle but golden brown on the outside.

Serve hot with noodles or warm Lemon Couscous Salad on p131.

serves 6

conventional oven
Fry over a high heat on the hob.

swiss beef pie with crispy filo topping

I love serving this at informal gatherings of family or friends. You could substitute the fennel with onions, if preferred.

❅ Not suitable for freezing.

1 tablespoon oil
1 head fennel, core removed, coarsely chopped
1kg (2.2lb) lean minced beef
2 cloves garlic, crushed
1 tablespoon flour
1 x 400g (14oz) tin chopped tomatoes
2 tablespoons tomato purée
1 teaspoon sugar
250g (9oz) courgettes, cut into batons
2 x 150g packs Boursin cheese
6 sheets of filo pastry
melted butter

Butter a shallow ovenproof dish about 2.1 litres (3½ pints) capacity.

Heat the oil in a non-stick frying pan on boiling plate. Fry the fennel for a couple of minutes. Add the mince to the pan and brown, stir in the garlic and sprinkle over the flour. Stir in the chopped tomatoes, tomato purée and sugar and season with salt and pepper. Bring to the boil, cover and transfer to the simmering oven for about 35–45 minutes until the mince is tender.

Cook the courgette batons in boiling salted water for about 2 minutes on the boiling plate, drain and refresh in cold water until stone cold.

Spread half the mince over the base of the ovenproof dish. Dollop the cheese over the top of the mince and scatter over the cooked courgette batons. Season with salt and pepper. Pour over the remaining mince ensuring all the courgettes and cheese are covered.

Brush each sheet of filo with melted butter. Scrunch each sheet into a rosette shape and sit on top of the mince, continue with the remaining sheets of filo. Brush the filo with more melted butter.

Slide onto the grid shelf on the floor of the roasting oven, with the cold sheet on the second set of runners, for about 35 minutes until golden brown and piping hot in the centre.

Serve hot with a dressed salad or some vegetables.

serves 6

conventional oven
Cook the mince over a low heat on the hob for about 45 minutes. Slide the completed dish into a preheated oven 180C/160C Fan/Gas 4 for about 40 minutes, if getting too brown cover with foil.

chilli with sour cream and cheese

This makes a great, easy party dish. Just serve with rice or tacos. The cheese and sour cream are the final essential finishing touches and are not to be forgotten! This is quite a mild chilli, so add more powder to taste if you prefer it hotter.

❄ Freezes well.

1 tablespoon oil
1 large onion, finely chopped
900g (2lb) minced beef
2 tablespoons mild chilli powder
1 tablespoon cumin powder
1 x 400g (14oz) tin chopped tomatoes
2 tablespoons tomato purée
1 tablespoon redcurrant jelly
1 x 400g (14oz) tin red kidney beans, drained and rinsed
salt and pepper

to serve
sour cream
Red Leicester cheese, grated

Heat the oil in large frying pan on the boiling plate. Add the onion and fry for a couple of minutes. Add the mince and continue to fry until brown. Sprinkle in the chilli powder and cumin powder and stir. Pour in the tomatoes, quarter-fill the empty tomato tin with water and add this to the mince. Add the remaining ingredients, season with salt and pepper and bring to boil.

Cover and transfer to the simmering oven for about 1 hour until the mince is tender. Serve hot with a dollop of sour cream and the grated cheese.

serves 6

conventional oven
Cook the mince on a low heat on the hob for about an hour until tender.

the classic steak

My favourite cut of steak is fillet – tender and succulent, by far the best cut of beef for steaks in my opinion. The amount of cooking time for any steak will depend on how thick it is; fillet steak is generally much thicker than sirloin or rump steak. It's best to cut a fillet steak to no more than about 3cm thick so that it can be cooked quickly without it toughening up.

I would suggest about a 175g (6oz) 3cm (1$\frac{1}{4}$ inch) thick fillet steak per person.

Heat a grill pan or non-stick frying pan on the boiling plate until piping hot. Coat each side of the steak with oil and fry for about 2 minutes on each side for rare, 3 minutes on each side on the boiling plate for medium, and for well done: 3 minutes on one side on the boiling plate and then transfer to the simmering plate for a further 4 minutes. Of course if you like your steak done very well done you can cook it for longer. After cooking, rest the steaks for a few minutes before serving.

If preferred you can cook your steak on the floor of the roasting oven. Preheat the grill pan directly on the floor of the roasting oven for about 5 minutes until piping hot. Cook the steaks as described above, turning over halfway through the cooking time, keeping the grill pan on the floor of the roasting oven. Rest the steaks for a few minutes before serving.

a few easy sauce ideas

red wine and mushroom sauce

While the steaks are resting, add 1 tablespoon of oil to the pan, add 50g (2oz) of sliced button mushrooms and sauté them on the boiling plate for a few minutes. Add 150 ml (1/4 pint) of both beef stock and red wine and reduce on the boiling plate by half to thicken.

tomato and basil sauce

While the steaks are resting, add 4 tablespoons of passata to the pan, with 1 tablespoon of sun-dried tomato paste and 1 teaspoon of sugar, a dash of Worcestershire sauce and boil for a few minutes on the boiling plate. Just before serving add 2 tablespoons of torn fresh basil leaves.

creamy peppercorn and brandy sauce

Crush some black peppercorns and brush either side of the steak with oil and press on the peppercorns. Continue cooking the steaks (see opposite). While the steaks are resting add about 3 tablespoons of brandy to the pan and reduce for a minute on the boiling plate, stir in 4 tablespoons of double cream and boil for a couple more minutes. Serve with the steak.

shallot and herb sauce

While the steaks are resting, add 3 finely chopped shallots to the pan and fry for a couple of minutes, stir in 3 tablespoons of full-fat crème fraîche and just before serving add 2 tablespoons of chopped fresh parsley and the same amount of fresh tarragon.

mini beef wellies with whisky and horseradish sauce

Only fillet steak will do for this recipe! Also be sure to roll the pastry very thinly to allow it to crisp during the short cooking time. The steaks can be wrapped and the sauce made up to 24 hours ahead.

❄ Freezes well, raw with the pastry wrapped round.

1 tablespoon oil
6 thick fillet steaks, about 150g (5oz) in weight each and about 4cm (1½") thick
1 x 375g packet ready-rolled puff pastry
3 teaspoons creamed horseradish sauce
a little beaten egg

whisky and horseradish sauce
1 small onion, finely chopped
300ml (½ pint) beef stock
150ml (¼ pint) whisky
1 x 200ml tub full-fat crème fraîche
2 teaspoons creamed horseradish
salt and pepper

Heat the oil in a non-stick frying pan on the boiling plate until very hot. Fry the steaks for 10 seconds on each side and a little less around the edges until sealed. Set aside to cool.

To make the sauce: fry the onion in the unwashed frying pan for a few minutes on the boiling plate. Add the stock and whisky and boil for a few minutes until reduced by a third. Stir in the crème fraîche and horseradish, season with salt and pepper. Sieve and discard the onion.

Cut off a third of the pastry and freeze the remainder for another time. Roll the pastry on a floured surface until very thin. Cut 12 strips from the pastry, about 1cm x 18cm (½" x 7") so it is long enough to wrap round the steaks.

Season the cooled steaks with salt and pepper and spread the top of each steak with half a teaspoon of horseradish. Take two strips of pastry and wrap them around the steaks in a cross shape, so the joins are underneath. The pastry underneath should just join but not overlap, so break off any excess.

(continued on page 110)

(continued from page 108)

Arrange on a baking sheet, brush the pastry with egg glaze and slide the sheet onto the top set of runners of the roasting oven for about 10 minutes, or until the pastry is golden brown and the steak is cooked rare. Leave them to rest for a few minutes before serving.

Serve with the hot sauce.

serves 6

conventional oven
Seal the steaks in a frying pan on the hob. Sit the wellies on a preheated hot baking sheet in a preheated oven 200C/180C Fan/Gas 6 for about 10 minutes until the pastry is crisp.

lamb pompeii

This is one of the best ways I know to casserole lamb – it's based on a recipe given to me by two close friends, Trish and Colin, who claim to have first come across it in a country pub some 40 years ago! Perfect with buttery mash.

❄ Freezes well.

2 tablespoons oil
450g (1lb) shoulder of lamb, cut into 3cm (1½") cubes
450g (1lb) leg of lamb, cut into 3cm (1½") cubes
6 shallots, peeled, kept whole
2 medium carrots, cut into thin batons
4 small sticks celery, sliced thinly on the diagonal
3 tablespoons flour
1 tablespoon Dijon mustard
2 tablespoons tomato ketchup
2 tablespoons brown sugar
450ml (¾ pint) good stock
75 ml cider vinegar
3 teaspoons capers

Heat the oil in a non-stick deep frying pan or casserole dish on the boiling plate. Add all the lamb and brown all over (you may need to do this in batches). Using a slotted spoon, transfer the lamb to a plate and set aside.

Add the shallots, carrot and celery to the pan and fry on the boiling plate for few minutes. Return the lamb to the pan, sprinkle in the flour and blend in the remaining ingredients, stirring well. Bring to the boil, season, cover and transfer to the simmering oven for about 1½–2 hours or until the lamb is tender.

Serve hot.

serves 6

conventional oven
Cook in a preheated oven 165C/145C Fan/Gas 3 for about 1½–2 hours or until the lamb is tender.

easter pot roast lamb

This is the perfect easy roast with no last minute gravy to make as the lamb is cooked in its own sauce. For maximum ease use mint sauce from a jar, but only use the best – the cheaper ones can be a little over vinegary.

❄ Not suitable for freezing

2 tablespoons oil
1.8kg (3lb) leg of lamb, on the bone

3 red onions, sliced
3 cloves garlic, crushed
300ml (½ pint) red wine
2 tablespoons Worcestershire sauce
150 ml (¼ pint) water
1 x 175g (7oz) tin of chopped tomatoes
2 tablespoons redcurrant jelly
2 good tablespoons mint sauce
salt and pepper
4 large sprigs fresh rosemary

Heat one tablespoon of the oil in large deep casserole dish on the boiling plate. Seal the lamb on all sides till golden brown. Remove from the pan and set aside.

Heat the rest of the oil and add the onions and garlic to the pan and fry on the boiling plate for a few minutes. Stir in the wine, Worcestershire sauce, water, chopped tomatoes, redcurrant jelly and mint sauce. Stir and bring to the boil, season with salt and pepper. Return the lamb to the pan and arrange the rosemary sprigs around. Bring to the boil, cover, and transfer to the simmering oven for about 3½ – 4 hours or until the lamb is just done but still pink in the middle, turn over halfway through.

Remove the lamb, cover with foil and set aside to rest. Allow the sauce to reduce on the boiling plate without the lid for about 5 minutes. If the lamb seems a little too sharp from the mint sauce then just stir in little more redcurrant jelly to sweeten.

Carve the lamb and serve with the sauce.

serves 6

conventional oven
Brown the lamb over a high heat. Continue as above, cover and transfer to a preheated oven 160C/140C Fan/Gas 3 for about 3–3½ hours until the lamb is done, but pink in the middle. Reduce the sauce, uncovered, over a high heat and serve with the carved lamb.

rosemary-crusted lamb with orange sauce

A rack of lamb is such a delicious cut, so tender and so quick to roast. Ensure the chine bone has been removed or has been cut right through from under the chops by the butcher, otherwise carving will prove difficult.

❄ Not suitable for freezing.

4 tablespoons fresh rosemary, chopped
rind of 1 orange
1 tablespoon runny honey
salt and pepper
2 racks of lamb, 7 chops in each, French trimmed

orange sauce
150 ml (¼ pint) red wine
150 ml (¼ pint) orange juice
2 teaspoons of cornflour
1 good tablespoon redcurrant jelly

Mix the rosemary, orange rind and honey together in a bowl, season with salt and pepper. Spread the rosemary paste over the skinned side of each rack and arrange paste-side up in a small roasting tin with the bones facing inwards. Slide the tin onto the second set of runners in the roasting oven for about 15–20 minutes (the lamb should be pink). Transfer the lamb onto a plate, cover in foil and leave to rest.

To make the sauce: mix the cornflour with a little cold orange juice, pour the remaining orange juice and red wine into the juices in the roasting tin, add the slaked cornfour and whisk till smooth. Whisk in the redcurrant jelly. Slide the tin onto the floor of the roasting oven for about 5 minutes until bubbling and thickened slightly.

Carve the lamb between the chops and serve with the orange sauce.

serves 4–6

conventional oven
Roast in a preheated oven 200C/180C Fan/Gas 6 for 15 minutes until just pink. Make the sauce on the hob as you would gravy.

shepherd's pie with squash topping

Sometimes there is nothing nicer than a comforting shepherd's pie – I like to add tomato to the mince and finish it off with a topping of potato and the unusual addition of squash.

❄ Freezes well without the topping.

1 tablespoon oil
1 large onion, finely chopped
1 large carrot, finely chopped
1kg (2.2lb) lean lamb mince
1 tablespoon of flour
150 ml ($^1/_4$ pint) lamb or beef stock
1 x 14oz tin chopped tomatoes
3 good tablespoons tomato purée
1 tablespoon redcurrant jelly
salt and pepper

1kg (2.2lb) potatoes, peeled
about 750g (1lb 2oz) butternut squash, peeled
butter and milk for mashing

You will need an ovenproof dish about 2.1 litre ($3^1/_2$ pint) capacity.

Heat the oil on the boiling plate in a large non-stick frying pan. Add the onions and carrots and fry for a minute. Add the mince, and fry on boiling plate until browned.

Sprinkle in the flour and blend in the stock, tomatoes, tomato purée and redcurrant jelly and bring to the boil, season with salt and pepper. Cover and transfer to the simmering oven for about 50 minutes until the meat is tender. Once cooked, spoon into an ovenproof deep dish and set aside.

To make the topping: cut the potato and squash into small even-sized cubes. Boil in salted water on the boiling plate until tender. Drain the potatoes and add the butter and milk, mash until smooth. Season.

Spoon the mash over the mince and spread evenly. Brush with a little melted butter. Slide onto the grid shelf on the floor of the roasting oven for about 40 minutes until golden brown and bubbling.

serves 6

conventional oven
Cook the mince on the hob. Place the completed dish in a preheated oven 200C/ 180C Fan/Gas 6 for about 40 minutes until golden brown and bubbling.

herbed pork and apple en croute

Bought puff pastry is excellent nowadays and helps make the impressively pretty dish an instant and easy classic.

❄ Freezes well raw and rolled.

filling
350g (12oz) good quality sausages
150g (5oz) mature Cheddar cheese, grated
2 small dessert apples, peeled and chopped into small cubes
3 tablespoons fresh parsley, chopped
1 tablespoon fresh thyme leaves
salt and pepper

1 x 375g ready-rolled puff pastry
1 egg, beaten
50g (2oz) sun-blushed tomatoes, snipped in half

Make a slit along the sausages and remove the skin, tip the meat into a bowl. Add the remaining filling ingredients and season with salt and pepper. Mix together using your hands.

Roll the pastry a little larger to 23cm x 30cm (9" x 12"). Spoon half the filling along the centre, leaving a 4cm (1½") gap of pastry at the ends and about 7cm (3") gap at the sides. Sprinkle over the sun-blushed tomatoes, and spoon the remaining filling on top, press with your hands to form an even shape. Using a small sharp knife, slice at 2cm (1") intervals along the sides and plait the pastry over the sausage meat. Brush with the beaten egg and place on a baking sheet.

Slide the tin onto the floor of the roasting oven for about 10 minutes until the pastry base is golden brown and then put onto the grid shelf on the floor for a further 30 minutes with the cold sheet on the second set of runners. Bake until crispy, golden brown and cooked through.

serves 6

conventional oven
Place on a very hot preheated baking sheet in oven 180C/160C Fan/Gas 4 for about 40 minutes, if getting too brown, cover with foil.

quick pork fillet with lime and thyme

This really couldn't be quicker or easier. The sauce is fairly thin so serve with rice or mash to mop up the juices.

❄ Not suitable for freezing.

1 tablespoon oil
450g (1lb) pork fillet, sliced into long thin strips
100g (4oz) button mushrooms, thinly sliced
1 small thin leek, thinly sliced
150ml ($\frac{1}{4}$ pint) apple juice
150ml ($\frac{1}{4}$ pint) stock
150ml ($\frac{1}{4}$ pint) double cream
salt and pepper
2 tablespoons fresh thyme leaves
2 tablespoons fresh lime juice

Heat the oil on the boiling plate and fry the pork until golden brown. Remove with a slotted spoon and set aside.

Add the mushrooms and leeks to the pan and fry for a few minutes on the boiling plate. Pour in the apple juice and stock and reduce by half, pour in the cream. Return the pork to the pan, season with salt and pepper, and simmer for about 8 minutes until the pork is tender.

Stir in the lime juice and thyme, check the seasoning and serve.

serves 4

conventional oven
Follow recipe as above. Cook over a high heat on the hob.

lower froyle ginger pork

I created this dish whilst staying with friends in the village of Lower Froyle in Hampshire. In order to save them cooking I raided their fridge and cupboards and devised this recipe. Use either loin steaks or pork fillet.

❄ Not suitable for freezing.

1 tablespoon oil
4 pork loin steaks, cut into thin strips
1 tablespoon honey
6 spring onions, finely sliced
about 3cm (1$\frac{1}{2}$") fresh ginger, grated
1 good tablespoon ground ginger
1 x 400g (14oz) tin coconut milk
1 x 170g (7oz) tin chopped tomatoes
salt and pepper
2 teaspoons balsamic vinegar

Heat the oil in large non-stick frying pan on boiling plate. Add the pork strips and fry for a minute or two. Add the honey and continue to fry until golden brown. Remove using a slotted spoon and set aside.

Add the spring onion and ginger to the pan and fry for a minute. Sprinkle in the ginger powder and fry for a further minute, stirring. Add the coconut milk, chopped tomatoes and season. Bring to the boil. Return the pork to the pan, and continue to boil uncovered for about 5 minutes, stirring from time to time until the pork is cooked and sauce has thickened slightly.

Stir in the balsamic vinegar and serve piping hot.

serves 4

conventional oven
Cook on the hob as above.

easy
vegetarian
and vegetables

cooking potatoes and vegetables

boiling potatoes

For best results: boil them in the oven – not only does this preserve the heat in the Aga by keeping the lids down, but it's also kinder to the potato as it cooks in a half simmer, half steam. Cut into even-sized pieces. Sit in a pan, cover with cold salted water. Bring to the boil on the boiling plate and boil for about 5 minutes (if too ferocious slide onto the simmering plate). Drain completely, return to the pan and cover with a lid, steam in the simmering oven for double the time you would normally boil them.

mashing potatoes

Cook as above and then add milk and butter, mash. Season with salt and pepper and any other flavouring, if liked.

roasting potatoes

Par-boil the potatoes before roasting – boil in salted water for about 4 minutes. Drain and shake in the colander to fluff up. Heat some fat in the roasting tin directly on the floor of the roasting oven for about 5 minutes until piping hot. Add the par-boiled potatoes and return to floor of the roasting oven for about an hour (depending on size of pieces) shaking occasionally. If the potatoes stick a little, this is because they are not completely crisp so leave them for a few more minutes and they will then release from the tin. Do not use too much fat for roast potatoes otherwise they will go soggy. If the potatoes are not getting brown enough, drain off some fat! The best fat to use is goose or duck fat, but sunflower or vegetable oil is also good – do not use butter as it will burn.

jacket potatoes

Put them in the roasting oven (you don't even need to put them in a tin!) and roast for about an hour or so depending on the size. If you are in a hurry, cut them in half, they will take half the time.

root vegetables

Bring to the boil from cold on the boiling plate, cover, boil for about 5 minutes, drain, cover and transfer to simmering oven for double the amount of time you would normally boil them on top. You can of course boil them on the top as you would on a conventional hob but you will lose heat from the Aga – it depends if you need to cook again after the meal.

green vegetables

Place in a pan of boiling salted water and boil on top without a lid until tender.

mushroom soufflé tarts

These are really scrummy: perfect as a starter or a light supper.

❄ Not suitable for freezing.

4 sheets of filo pastry
melted butter

soufflé
50g (2oz) butter
50g (2oz) flour
200ml (7floz) milk
2 eggs, separated
knob of butter
100g (4oz) chestnut mushrooms, thinly sliced
8 spring onions, finely chopped
2 cloves garlic, crushed
1 tablespoon soy sauce
salt and pepper
75g (3oz) mature Cheddar cheese, grated
2 tablespoons, fresh parsley, chopped

You will need six buttered ramekins or a 6-hole deep muffin tin.

Brush each sheet of filo with melted butter and cut into three, widthways.
Place 2 sheets on top of each other to form a cross shape. Push each cross into
a ramekin to cover the base and sides.

To make the soufflé: melt the butter in a pan on the boiling plate, whisk in the
flour and gradually add the milk, whisking all the time. Stir in the egg yolks and
season with salt and pepper then stir in half the cheese and the parsley and set
aside to slightly cool. Whisk the egg whites until stiff and fold them into the
cooled egg mixture. Heat the butter in a frying pan and add the mushrooms,
spring onions and garlic and fry for few minutes until golden. Add the soy sauce
and season with salt and pepper. Stir into the soufflé mixture.

Divide the mixture between the ramekins and sprinkle with the remaining cheese.
Sit them on a baking sheet and slide it onto the floor of the roasting oven for about
8 minutes, then slide onto the top set of runners for about another 4 minutes or
until they are a light golden brown. Serve hot with a dressed salad.

serves 6

conventional oven
Bake in a preheated oven 200C/180C Fan/Gas 6 for 10–12 minutes.

chickpea and spinach filo tart

A simple and delicious tart, needing only the addition of a lightly dressed salad.

❄ Not suitable for freezing.

5 sheets of filo pastry
melted butter

1 tablespoon oil
225g (8oz) baby spinach
1 x 390g tin artichoke hearts, cut in half
1 x 400g (14oz) tin chickpeas, drained
2 large cloves garlic, crushed
salt and pepper
1 x 250g (9oz) tub Ricotta cheese
100g (4oz) mature Cheddar, grated

Brush each sheet of filo with melted butter. Line the base and sides of a deep 23cm (9") spring form tin with the filo in two layers.

Heat the oil in non-stick frying pan on the boiling plate. Add the spinach and fry until wilted. Stir in the artichokes, chickpeas and garlic, season with salt and pepper and fry for a couple of minutes. Tip the mixture into a bowl to cool slightly and then stir in the Ricotta and half the Cheddar. Spoon the mixture into the tin and sprinkle over the remaining cheddar.

Slide the tin onto the grid shelf on the floor of the roasting oven for 10 minutes then remove the shelf and continue to cook the tart directly on the floor for a further 10 minutes until golden brown and the pastry is crisp.

Serve hot with a dressed salad.

serves 4–6

conventional oven
Heat a baking sheet until very hot in a preheated oven 200C/180C Fan/Gas 6 and bake directly on the hot baking sheet for about 20 minutes until golden brown.

oven-roasted courgettes with goats' cheese

Serve the courgettes either simply with a salad or as an accompanying dish. They can be made up to 12 hours ahead.

❄ Not suitable for freezing.

2 medium courgettes
150g (5oz) soft goats' cheese
4 teaspoons grainy mustard
little paprika

Cut the courgettes in half lengthways and remove the seeds using a teaspoon. Then cut them in half widthways so you have 8 scooped out pieces of courgette.

Fill each piece with half a teaspoon of mustard and then fill with goats' cheese. Sprinkle with paprika and arrange snugly in a greased ovenproof dish or roasting tin.

Slide onto the grid shelf on the floor of the roasting oven for about 30 minutes until the courgette is just tender.

serves 2–4

conventional oven
Bake in a preheated oven 200C/C Fan/Gas 6 for about 30 minutes until tender.

lemon couscous salad

You can either serve the couscous cold as a salad or warm as an accompaniment. To serve warm, cover the bowl in clingfilm and heat through in the simmering oven for about 15 minutes.

✳ Not suitable for freezing.

225g (8oz) couscous
400 ml (14floz) boiling water
1 large carrot, peeled and coarsely grated
3 sticks of celery, cut into small dice
50g (2oz) sultanas
1 x 200g packet feta cheese, cut into 1cm ($1/2$") cubes
juice of 1 lemon
2 tablespoons olive oil
4 tablespoons fresh basil, roughly chopped

Measure the couscous into a heatproof bowl. Pour the measured water into an empty Aga kettle and boil on the boiling plate. Pour the boiling water over the couscous. Cover in clingfilm and set aside for about 5–10 minutes until all the water has been absorbed.

Fluff up with a fork and add all the remaining ingredients. Stir and season with salt and pepper.

serves 4–8

parsnip and potato dauphinois

This is a variation of the old classic Pommes Dauphinois, but with the addition of parsnip. There is often a debate as to whether it should be made with all cream or all stock, though I prefer to avoid the argument and use half and half instead!

❈ Not suitable for freezing.

550g (1lb 4oz) potatoes, peeled, cut into very thin slices
salt and pepper
350g (12oz) parsnips, peeled, cut into very thin slices
6 spring onions, coarsely chopped
150 ml ($1/_4$ pint) vegetable stock
150 ml ($1/_4$ pint) double cream
15g ($1/_2$oz) Parmesan cheese, grated

You will need a 1.5 litre ($2^1/_2$ pint) shallow dish, buttered.

Blanch the potato slices in salted water for 3–4 minutes. Drain and refresh them in cold water until cold. Then do the same with the parsnips and spring onions together and set aside separate from the potatoes.

Arrange half the potatoes in the base of the dish and then place all the parsnips and spring onions on top. Top with the remaining potatoes, seasoning between the layers. Pour the stock and cream over and sprinkle with the grated cheese.

Slide onto the second set of runners in the roasting oven and bake for about 50–55 minutes until golden brown and tender. Serve hot.

serves 6

conventional oven
Bake in preheated oven 200C/180C Fan/Gas 6 for about an hour until golden brown and tender.

spinach enchiladas with tomato sauce

A Mexican inspired light lunch or supper dish. Can be made up to 12 hours ahead.

❄ Not suitable for freezing.

1 tablespoon oil
1 onion, thinly sliced
225g (8oz) button mushrooms, sliced
225g (8oz) fresh spinach
2 cloves garlic, crushed
salt and pepper
6 fajita wraps
200g (7oz) Feta cheese, cut into cubes the size of a dice
1 x 500g carton passatta
1 tablespoon Worcestershire sauce
25g (1oz) fresh Parmesan cheese, finely grated
2 tablespoons fresh parsley, chopped

Heat the oil in a large non-stick frying pan on the boiling plate. Add the onion and mushrooms and fry for a few minutes. Add the spinach and garlic and fry for another couple of minutes, stirring continuously, season with salt and pepper. Set aside to cool.

Lay out the fajitas on the work surface. Divide the spinach mixture into six and spoon a portion down the centre of each one. Arrange the feta along the top of the spinach mixture and roll the fajita up from the long end, in a cigar shape. Arrange in a single layer in an ovenproof dish.

Mix the passatta with the Worcestershire sauce, season and pour over the fajitas in the dish. Sprinkle over the Parmesan cheese.

Slide onto the second set of runners in the roasting oven for about 30 minutes, cover with foil after 15 minutes if getting too brown.

Serve hot sprinkled with chopped parsley.

serves 6

conventional oven
Bake in a preheated oven 200C/180C Fan/Gas 6 for about 30 minutes until piping hot.

roasted baby new potatoes with garlic and rosemary

Fantastic roast potatoes the easy way – no par-boiling required!

❋ Not suitable for freezing.

900g (2lb) baby new potatoes, skin on
2 tablespoons goose fat
3 cloves garlic, peeled
1 large sprig fresh rosemary

Cut the potatoes in half lengthways, if very small leave whole. Spoon the goose fat into a small roasting tin and slide onto the floor of the roasting oven for about 5 minutes to become hot.

When the fat is piping hot, tip in potatoes, garlic cloves and sprig of rosemary. Shake the tin so the potatoes are coated in the hot fat and return the tin to the floor of the roasting oven for about 35 minutes until tender and crispy.

Discard the rosemary and garlic and serve potatoes immediately.

serves 6

conventional oven
Roast in a preheated oven 200C/180C Fan/Gas 6 for about 30 minutes until tender and crisp.

spicy hot vegetable curry

This is a curry with a kick! Once all the preparation has been done it's a breeze to make. Good either as an accompanying dish or as a main course with Basmati rice.

❄ Not suitable for freezing.

1 tablespoon oil
1 onion, finely chopped
about 3cm (1.5") fresh ginger, grated
1–2 small red chillies, seeds removed, finely chopped
2 aubergines cut into 2cm (1") cubes
1 large potato, peeled cut into 2cm (1") cubes
2 small carrots, peeled, coarsely grated
2 tablespoons medium curry powder
2 teaspoons paprika
2 x 400g (14oz) tins chopped tomatoes
2 tablespoons mango chutney
juice of $\frac{1}{2}$ a lemon

Heat the oil in large non-stick frying pan on the boiling plate. Add the onion, ginger and chilli and fry for a couple of minutes.

Add the remaining vegetables to the pan, stir, sprinkle in the spices and fry for a minute. Stir in the tomatoes and season. Bring to the boil, cover and transfer to simmering oven for about $1\frac{1}{4}$ hours until potatoes are just tender.

Stir in the mango chutney and lemon juice, serve hot with rice.

serves 4–6

conventional oven
Cook in a preheated oven 180C/160C Fan/Gas 4 for about 1–1$\frac{1}{4}$ hours until the potatoes are just tender.

sweet potato and lentil pie

This lightly spiced vegetable pie makes the perfect simple lunch accompanied with a salad or as a main course served with extra vegetables.

❄ Not suitable for freezing.

1.2 kg (2½lb) sweet potatoes, peeled
175g (6oz) Gruyère cheese, grated
2 tablespoons oil
450g (1lb) white cup mushrooms, quartered
2 x 400g (14oz) tins lentils, drained and rinsed
2 cloves garlic, crushed
1 tablespoon dried cumin
salt and pepper

You will need a shallow ovenproof dish – about 28cm (11") diameter, buttered.

Cut the potatoes into even-sized chunks and boil them in salted water until tender. Drain, mash and season with salt and pepper. Stir in half the cheese while the mash is still hot.

Heat the oil in a non-stick frying pan on the boiling plate. Add the mushrooms and fry for a minute or two. Stir in the lentils, garlic and cumin and season with salt and pepper. Tip into the greased dish.

Spoon over the mash and spread with a palette knife so all the lentil mixture is covered. Sprinkle with the remaining cheese.

Slide onto the top set of runners in the roasting oven for about 15–20 minutes until tinged brown and piping hot.

serves 6

conventional oven
Bake in a preheated oven 200C/180C Fan/Gas 6 for about 20 minutes.

easy
cakes, puddings and desserts

mint chocolate traybake

Traybakes really are the easiest cakes to make, as one tray serves so many people. This quantity fills a small Aga roasting tin but you could, of course, double the recipe to serve in the large Aga roasting tin. Peppermint extract is sold in all good supermarkets and delis – it is very strong, so go steady!

❄ Freezes well un-iced.

4 tablespoons cocoa
4 tablespoons hot water
225g (8oz) butter, soft
225g (8oz) caster sugar
2 teaspoons baking powder
4 eggs
300g (10oz) self raising flour

icing
225g (8oz) icing sugar
2$\frac{1}{2}$ tablespoons cold water
1 teaspoon peppermint extract
25g (1oz) Bournville chocolate, shaved using a vegetable peeler

You will need a small Aga roasting tin, lined with foil and greased.

Measure the cocoa into a large mixing bowl. Blend with hot water to form a paste. Add the remaining cake ingredients and mix together until smooth. Pour into the prepared tin.

2-oven AGA
Slide onto the lowest set of runners in the roasting oven with the cold sheet on the second set of runners. Bake for about 25–30 minutes until it begins to shrink away from the sides of the tin and is springy to the touch.

3- and 4-oven AGA
Slide onto the lowest set of runners in the baking oven. Bake for about 25–30 minutes until it begins to shrink away from the sides of the tin and is springy to the touch. If getting too brown slide the cold sheet onto the second set of runners.

To make the icing: sieve the icing sugar over a bowl and mix in the water and peppermint essence. Once the cake has cooled, pour over the icing and using a palette knife spread to the corners. Sprinkle over the chocolate shavings.

cuts into 16 pieces

conventional oven
Bake in a preheated oven 180C/160C Fan/Gas 4 for about 30 minutes.

greek yoghurt and honey cake

I love this yoghurt cake, it's very similar in texture to a Madeira cake. The icing makes it extra delicious but do please keep it in the fridge and not in a tin.

❄ Freezes well un-iced.

75g (3oz) butter, soft
300g (11oz) caster sugar
3 eggs, separated
1–2 teaspoons vanilla extract
1 x 200g (7oz) tub Greek yoghurt
225g (8oz) self-raising flour

honey and yoghurt icing
1 x 200g (7oz) tub Greek yoghurt
2 tablespoons runny honey

Lightly grease 2 x 20cm (8") loose-bottomed round sandwich tins and line the bases with a circle of non-stick baking parchment.

Mix the butter, sugar, egg yolks, vanilla and yoghurt into a large mixing bowl and beat until smooth.

Whisk the egg whites until stiff like cloud. Stir one spoonful of egg white into the cake mixture. Cut and fold the remaining egg whites into the mixture taking care not to knock the air out of the whites. Sieve in the flour and gently stir into the cake mixture.

Spoon evenly between the cake tins, levelling the top.

2-oven AGA
Slide onto the grid shelf on the floor of the roasting oven with the cold shelf on the second set of runners. Bake for about 20 minutes until golden brown and shrinking away from the sides of the tin.

3- and 4-oven AGA
Slide onto the grid shelf on the floor of the baking oven for about 20 minutes until golden brown and shrinking away from the sides of the tin. If getting too brown, slide the cold shelf onto the second set of runners.

(continued on page 146)

(continued from page 144)

Leave to cool in the tins. Turn out and remove the paper. Mix 1 tablespoon of honey with the Greek yoghurt and spread half over the base of one cake and place the other cake on top. Spoon the remaining icing on top of the cake and spread with a palette knife. Drizzle the remaining tablespoon of honey over the top in lines and using a skewer or handle of a teaspoon, drag in the opposite direction to honey lines to form a feather pattern. Transfer to the fridge until serving.

serves 6–8

conventional oven
Bake in a preheated oven 180C/160C Fan/Gas 4 for about 20–25 minutes.

chocolate fruit cake

A lovely alternative to a traditional Christmas cake – I have added chocolate thus ensuring that it will be loved by all the family! Keeps for up to 6 weeks, wrapped in foil in the fridge.

❄ Freezes well.

225g (8oz) ready-to-eat dried apricots, snipped
225g (8oz) butter, softened
225g (8oz) light muscovado sugar
175g (6oz) plain flour
50g (2oz) cocoa
4 large eggs
100g (4oz) glace cherries, cut into quarters and rinsed
225g (8oz) sultanas
zest and 2 tablespoons of 1 large orange

Grease and line a 20cm (8") deep round cake tin with a double layer of greaseproof.

Cream the butter and sugar together in a large mixing bowl. Add the remaining ingredients and continue to mix until well blended. Spoon the mixture into the prepared tin and spread out evenly.

Slide the tin onto the grid shelf on the floor of the roasting oven with the cold sheet on the second set of runners. Bake for about 30–35 minutes or until brown and beginning to set on top. Transfer the heated cold sheet to the simmering oven and sit the cake on top and bake for about 2 hours. Test with a skewer – the cake is done when the skewer comes out clean.

Set aside to cool in the tin and then carefully remove. Dust with icing sugar to serve or decorate with dried apricots and glaze.

cuts into 8–10 slices

conventional oven
Bake in a preheated oven 160C/140C Fan/Gas 3 for about $1\frac{1}{2}$ hours, you may need to cover with foil for the last 15 minutes if becoming too brown.

banana and chocolate chips loaf

A perfect recipe for when the bananas in the fruit bowl are over ripe and no one wants to eat them!

❄ Freezes well.

2 eggs
100g (4oz) self-raising flour
100g (4oz) soft butter
100g (4oz) caster sugar
$\frac{1}{2}$ teaspoon baking powder
1 over ripe large banana, mashed
25g (1oz) chocolate chips

Grease and line a 450g (1lb) loaf tin.

Measure all the ingredients, except the chocolate chips into a large mixing bowl and beat well until smooth. Stir in half the chocolate chips. Spoon into the lined tin and level the top, sprinkle over the remaining chocolate chips.

2-oven AGA
Sit the small grill rack in the lowest position in the small roasting tin and sit the loaf tin on top. Slide onto the lowest set of runners in the roasting oven with the cold shelf on the second set of runners for about 30–35 minutes until dark golden brown and shrinking away from the sides of the tin. If you find it's getting too brown you may need to change the cold sheet halfway through cooking.

3- and 4-oven AGA
Slide the loaf tin (no need for the roasting tin) onto the lowest set of runners in the baking oven for about 30–35 minutes. If the cake is getting too brown, slide the cold shelf on the second set of runners.

makes 6–8 slices

conventional oven
Bake in a preheated oven 180C/160C Fan/Gas 4 for about 35 minutes.

lemon victoria sandwich

A classic that is also lovely made with orange – replace the lemon zest with orange zest and the lemon curd with orange curd. Store in the fridge.

❅ Freezes well plain or filled.

225g (8 oz) butter, softened
225g (8 oz) caster sugar
4 eggs
225g (8 oz) self-raising flour
2 level teaspoons baking powder
grated zest of 1 lemon

filling and topping
About 4 tablespoons lemon curd
3 tablespoons half-fat crème fraîche
A little caster sugar

Lightly grease two 20 cm (8 inch) loose-bottomed sandwich tins and line the bases with a circle of non-stick baking parchment.

Measure all the cake ingredients into a large bowl and mix together until smooth. Divide the mixture evenly between the tins and level the top.

2-oven AGA
Slide the tins onto the grid shelf on the floor of the roasting oven, with the cold sheet on the second set of runners. Bake for about 20 minutes until well-risen and golden brown.

3- and 4-oven AGA
Slide tins onto the grid shelf on the floor of the baking oven for about 20 minutes until well risen and golden. If getting too brown slide the cold sheet onto the second set of runners.

Leave to cool in the tins. Turn out and remove the paper. Mix the lemon curd with the crème fraîche. Spread over the base of one cake and sandwich together with the other cake. Sprinkle the top with caster sugar.

conventional oven
Bake in a preheated oven 180C/160C Fan/Gas 4 for about 20 minutes.

smartie cookies

These brilliant cookies can be made any size you like, but be careful as they spread when cooking. For variety, use sultanas instead of Smarties.

❄ Freeze well.

225g (8oz) butter, soft
175g (6oz) caster sugar
100g (4oz) light muscovado sugar
2 eggs, beaten
300g (10oz) self-raising flour
175g (6oz) Smarties

Measure the softened butter and sugars into a large bowl and mix thoroughly until evenly blended. Gradually add the beaten eggs, beating well between each addition, finally fold in the flour.

Spoon a heaped tablespoon of the mixture onto greased baking trays, leaving room for the cookies to spread, about 8 per tray.

2-oven AGA
Slide onto the grid shelf on the floor of the roasting oven with the cold shelf on the second set of runners. Bake for about 8–10 minutes until golden brown. While they are still hot, press the Smarties into the top and set aside for the cookies to firm up.

3- and 4-oven AGA
Slide onto the grid shelf on the floor of the baking oven. Bake for about 8–10 minutes until golden brown, if getting too brown, slide the cold sheet on the second set of runners. While they are still hot, press the Smarties into the top and set aside for the cookies to firm up.

makes at least 20

conventional oven
Bake in a preheated oven 180C/160C Fan/Gas 3 for about 8–10 minutes.

Picture shows Smartie Cookies with White Chocolate and Cranberry Crispies (p153)

millionaire's apple cake

Named because it is so rich (and creamy) – also quite unusual as I have added cream to the sponge. No need to ice, just dust with icing sugar to serve.

❄ Freezes well.

100g (4oz) butter, soft
100g (4oz) light brown sugar
175g (6oz) self-raising flour
2 large eggs
100ml (4floz) pouring double cream
3 dessert apples, peeled and cut into cubes the size of a sugar lump
25g (1oz) sultanas
25g (1oz) Demerara sugar

You will need a small Aga roasting tin, line with foil and grease.

Measure the butter, sugar, flour, eggs and cream into a bowl and beat well until smooth. Stir in the apples and sultanas and tip the mixture into the lined tin and spread out evenly. Sprinkle over the Demerara sugar.

2-oven AGA
Slide onto the grid shelf on the floor of the roasting oven with the cold sheet on the second set of runners. Bake for about 30 minutes or until golden brown and shrinking away from the sides of the tin.

3- and 4-oven AGA
Slide onto the grid shelf on the floor of the baking oven. Bake for about 30 minutes or until golden brown and shrinking away from the sides of the tin. If getting too brown slide the cold sheet on the second set of runners halfway through.

Dust with icing sugar and serve cold or warm with a little more cream!

cuts into about 16 squares

conventional oven
Bake in a preheated oven 180C/160C Fan/Gas 4 for about 30 minutes.

white chocolate and cranberry crispies

Original and delicious and guaranteed to disappear from the biscuit tin in minutes!

❄ Not suitable for freezing.

1 x 200g (7oz) good quality white chocolate (Lindt is excellent)
50g (2oz) butter
3 tablespoons golden syrup
100g (4oz) rice crispies
100g (4oz) dried cranberries, coarsely chopped

Line a 30 cm x 23cm (12" x 9") Swiss roll tin with clingfilm.

Chop 50g (2oz) of the measured white chocolate into chunks the size of raisins. Measure the remaining chocolate into a bowl. Pour the golden syrup on top of the chocolate, add the butter and sit the bowl on the back of the Aga until melted, stirring occasionally.

Measure the rice crispies, cranberries and chunks of white chocolate into a bowl, pour over the melted chocolate mixture and stir.

Spoon the mixture into the tin and transfer to the fridge to set for minimum of an hour.

Tip out of the tin and cut into 16 pieces.

makes 16 biscuits

conventional oven
To melt the chocolate, measure into a bowl with the golden syrup and butter. Sit the bowl over a pan of gently simmering water and stir until melted.

apple and lemon brioche tartlets

These fantastic little tartlets are so quick to make and so divine to eat. I make them for dinner parties 12 hours ahead of time and then bake and glaze just before serving. Not suitable for freezing.

6 slices of a brioche loaf, about 1cm ($\frac{1}{2}$") thick
4 tablespoons full-fat cream cheese
2 tablespoons luxury lemon curd
1 tablespoon caster sugar
2 red skinned dessert apples, sliced with skin on into wafer thin slices
2 tablespoons apricot jam
2 tablespoons water

Remove the crusts from the brioche slices. Mix the cream cheese, lemon curd and sugar in a bowl and spread over the slices. Arrange the apple slices over the top of the cream cheese in a neat pattern. Place on a baking sheet. Slide the sheet onto the floor of the roasting oven for about 8–10 minutes until golden brown and crisp.

Heat the apricot jam and water in a saucepan on the boiling plate, whisking until hot and blended. Using a pastry brush, brush the jam over the sliced apple to glaze.

Serve warm, with added cream if liked.

serves 6

conventional oven
Sit the tarts on a preheated baking sheet in an oven 200C/180C Fan/Gas 6 for about 8 minutes.

roasted hazelnut and orange cake

A deep moist cake full of flavour which doesn't need an icing – just dust with icing sugar to serve.

❋ Freezes well.

100g (4oz) roasted hazelnuts, finely chopped
175g (6oz) self-raising flour
175g (6oz) soft butter
175g (6oz) light muscovado sugar
1 teaspoon baking powder
3 eggs
grated zest of 2 oranges

Grease a deep 20cm (8") round cake tin and line with a circle of paper.

Measure all the ingredients into a mixing bowl, and beat until smooth. Tip into the prepared tin.

2-oven AGA
Slide the tin onto the grid shelf on the floor of the roasting oven, with the cold sheet on the second set of runners. Bake for about 35 minutes until dark golden brown and shrinking away from the sides of the tin. If getting too brown, replace the cold sheet halfway.

3- and 4-oven AGA
Slide the tin onto the grid shelf on the floor of the baking oven. Bake for about 35 minutes until dark golden and shrinking away from the sides of the tin.
If getting too brown, slide the cold sheet onto the second set of runners.

cuts into 8 slices

conventional oven
Bake in a preheated oven 180C/160C Fan/Gas 4 for about 35 minutes.

lemon passion posset

A quick and refreshing dessert that will be loved by all. Can be made up to 24 hours ahead.

✳ Not suitable for freezing

600ml (1 pint) pouring double cream
100g (4oz) caster sugar
4 passion fruit
juice of 2 lemons

You will need 8 small coffee cups or shot glasses.

Pour the cream and sugar into a wide-based pan and bring to simmering point, stirring continuously for about 3 minutes until all the sugar has dissolved.

Remove from the heat and allow to cool slightly. Cut the passion fruit in half and scoop out the pips and juice. Sieve the pips over the pan until all the juice is in the pan and only pips remain in the sieve – discard the pips.

Pour the lemon juice into the pan and stir.

Pour the mixture into cups or shot glasses. Transfer to the fridge to set. Leave to set for a minimum of 4 hours.

serves 8

conventional oven
Heat the sugar and cream gently over low heat.

pineapple tarte tatin

This is a pineapple version of the classic apple tarte tatin. Many think a tatin is hard to make, but this is a misapprehension; follow the instructions below and you will discover that, to the contrary, it is one of the quickest of hot desserts that can be made. From weighing out to putting in the Aga, I once made this during the half time of an FA Cup Final!

❊ Not suitable for freezing

french pastry
175g (6oz) plain flour
100g (4oz) butter
25g (1oz) icing sugar
1 egg yolk

100g (4oz) butter
100g (4oz) Demerara sugar
1 x small fresh ripe pineapple

Grease a deep 20cm (8") round cake tin and line with a circle of paper.

To make the pastry: measure the flour and butter into a processor and whiz until like breadcrumbs. Add the sugar and egg and whiz again till combined into a ball. Wrap in clingfilm and leave to rest in the fridge while making the caramel.

To make the caramel: melt the butter and sugar in a pan on the simmering plate and stir until the butter has melted and the sugar has dissolved. Pour into the base of the tin.

Remove the skin from the pineapple, cut into quarters and remove the core. Cut into very thin even-sized pieces (all the same shape if possible). Arrange the pineapple slices in a spiral pattern over the caramel in the base of the tin. Continue to layer all the pineapple.

Roll the pastry out on a floured surface to the same size as the cake tin. Sit the pastry on top of the pineapple inside the tin.

Slide the tin onto the grid shelf on the floor of the roasting oven for about 25 minutes until bubbling and the pastry is golden brown and cooked. Remove from the oven and allow to cool for about 10 minutes.

Holding the pastry in place, tip the tin and pour the juices from the tin into a small saucepan. Boil the juices on the boiling plate for a few minutes until thickened. Invert the tarte tatin onto a serving dish with the pineapple on top and pastry underneath, pour over the thickened juices.

Serve warm with crème fraîche, cream or ice cream.

serves 6

conventional oven
Bake in a preheated oven 220C/200C Fan/Gas 7 for about 20–25 minutes until bubbling and the pastry is golden brown and cooked. Continue as above boiling the juices over a high heat until thickened.

indulgent chocolate and date torte

Rich, sweet and delicious. Serve warm or cold – if serving warm as a dessert, heat in the simmering oven for about 15 minutes before icing and then dust with icing sugar to serve.

❄ Freezes well without icing.

25g (1oz) cocoa
100g (4oz) Bournville chocolate
50g (2oz) butter
175g (6oz) caster sugar
100ml (4floz) water
225g (8oz) soft, pitted, dried dates, snipped into small pieces
4 egg whites
75g (3oz) self-raising flour, sieved

icing
100g (4oz) Bournville chocolate
25g (1oz) unsalted butter

Grease a 23cm (9") spring form or loose-bottomed deep cake tin, and line with a circle of paper.

Measure the cocoa, chocolate, butter and caster sugar into a saucepan with the water. Heat on the simmering plate, stirring until the chocolate and butter has melted and sugar has dissolved. Stir in the dates and set aside to cool slightly.

Whisk the egg whites with an electric hand whisk until stiff. Fold the cooled chocolate mixture into the egg whites until smooth. Then fold in the sieved flour until also smooth. Pour into the prepared tin and level the top.

2-oven AGA
Bake on the grid shelf on floor of roasting oven with the cold sheet on the second set of runners for about 30 minutes until set on top.

3- and 4-oven AGA
Bake on the grid shelf on the floor of roasting oven for about 30 minutes until set on top.

(continued on page 162)

(continued from page 160)

To make the icing: break the chocolate pieces into a bowl, add the butter and sit the bowl on the back of the Aga until the chocolate has melted, stir until smooth.

Using a palette knife release the cake from the edge of the tin and leave to cool a little in the tin. Remove from the tin and place on a plate. Blob the icing over the top and sides of the cake and smooth with a palette knife.

Dust with icing sugar and serve with crème fraîche or cream.

serves 6–8

conventional oven
Bake in a preheated oven 180C/160C Fan/Gas 4 for about 35 minutes until set.

lemon and lime tart

Tarte au citron with added limes. Serve warm or chilled. If preferred you can use bought sweet pastry for extra ease.

❄ Freezes well.

pastry
225g (8oz) plain flour
100g (4oz) butter
25g (1oz) caster sugar
1 egg, beaten
1–2 tablespoons water

filling
6 eggs
600ml (1 pint) double cream
grated rind and juice of 2 small lemons
grated rind and juice of 3 limes
300g (10oz) caster sugar

You will need a loose-bottomed 28cm (11") flan tin.

To make the pastry: measure the flour and butter into a processor and whiz until like breadcrumbs. Add the sugar, egg and water and whiz again till combined into a ball.

Roll out the pastry on a lightly floured work surface to about 5cm (3") bigger than the tart tin. Line the base and the sides of the tin and prick the base with a fork. Set aside in the fridge to rest.

Measure the filling ingredients into a bowl and whisk by hand until smooth.

Pour the filling mixture into the tin and slide onto the floor of the roasting oven for about 30–35 minutes until the filling is set and the pastry is golden brown and crisp. You may need to slide the cold shelf onto the second set of runners after about 20 minutes if it's getting too brown.

Serve dusted with icing sugar.

serves 8

conventional oven
Line the pastry tin with parchment paper and baking beans. Cook in a preheated oven 200C/180C Fan/Gas 6 for about 10 minutes. Remove the beans and paper and return the pastry shell to the oven at the same temperature for a further 5 minutes or until the pastry shell has dried out. To cook the completed tart, bake in a preheated oven 180C/160C Fan/Gas 4 for about 35 minutes until the filling is set.

chocca mocca mousse

The quickest chocolate mousse you will ever make – no gelatine and no raw eggs. It is outrageously indulgent, so serve in small coffee cups!

❋ Freezes well.

1 x 200g (7oz) bar Bournville chocolate
2 tablespoons instant coffee
150ml (¼ pint) double cream
1 x 9oz (250g) tub Mascarpone cheese, at room temperature

You will need 8 small coffee cups or shot glasses.

Roughly chop 2 squares of the Bournville bar, set aside.

Break the remaining chocolate into a bowl and pour over the cream, sit on the back of the Aga till melted, stir until smooth. Set aside to cool slightly.

Measure the coffee into a large mixing bowl and pour in 1 tablespoon of boiling water, mix together. Add the Mascarpone to the coffee and beat till smooth. Gradually add the melted chocolate and cream to the Mascarpone and whisk until smooth

Pour into coffee cups. Sprinkle chopped chocolate on top. Transfer to the fridge to set for a minimum of 2 hours.

Serve chilled.

serves 8

conventional oven
Melt the chocolate and cream in a bowl over gently simmering water. Stir until melted but don't allow to get too hot. If you are very careful you can melt the chocolate in the microwave, which is much quicker!

rhubarb and custard french flan

I absolutely adore desserts and this is one of my all time favourites. You can use bought sweet dessert pastry, if preferred.

❄ Freezes well cooked, but glaze to serve.

pastry
225g (8oz) plain flour
100g (4oz) butter
25g (1oz) caster sugar
1 egg yolk
1–2 tablespoons cold water

custard
3 eggs, beaten
300ml ($\frac{1}{2}$ pint) double cream
50g (2oz) caster sugar
1 teaspoon vanilla extract
1 x 250g tub Mascarpone cheese

2 x 400g (14oz) tins of rhubarb in syrup or 900g (2lb) stewed rhubarb (reserve some syrup)
4 tablespoons Demerara sugar

You will need a deep loose-bottomed 28cm (11") flan tin.

To make the pastry: measure the flour and butter into a processor and whiz until like breadcrumbs. Add the sugar, egg yolk and water and whiz again till combined into a ball.

Roll out the pastry on a lightly floured work surface to about 5cm (3") bigger than the tart tin. Line the base and sides of the tin and prick the base with a fork. Set aside in the fridge to rest.

Measure the custard ingredients into a bowl, and whisk by hand until smooth. Pour the custard into the tin. Arrange the rhubarb over the top and sprinkle with Demerara sugar.

Slide onto the floor of the roasting oven for about 25–30 minutes until the custard is just set. If getting too brown, slide the cold sheet onto the second set of runners.

(continued on page 174)

(continued from page 172)

Heat 4 tablespoons of the stewed rhubarb syrup (or from the tin) with a tablespoon of caster sugar. Dissolve the sugar and boil on the boiling plate for a few minutes to thicken a little. Using a pastry brush glaze the top of the tart.

Serve warm with crème fraîche.

serves 8

conventional oven
Line the pastry tin with parchment paper and baking beans. Cook in a preheated oven 200C/180C Fan/Gas 6 for about 10 minutes. Remove the beans and paper and return the pastry shell to the oven at the same temperature for a further 5 minutes, or until the pastry shell has dried out. To cook the completed tart, bake in a preheated oven 180C/160C Fan/Gas 4 for about 35 minutes until the filling is set.

triple berry pavlova

A classic recipe perfect for any occasion. The unfilled pavlova will keep for up to a month wrapped in clingfilm and foil and kept in a dry place.

4 egg whites
225g (8 oz) caster sugar
2 teaspoons cornflour
2 teaspoons white wine vinegar

filling
150ml (5 fl oz) whipping cream, whipped
1 x 200g tub Greek yoghurt
75g (3oz) fresh raspberries
75g (3oz) fresh blueberries
75g (3oz) fresh strawberries, quartered

Line a large flat baking tray with a sheet of non-stick baking parchment and mark with a 23cm (9") circle.

Whisk the egg whites with an electric whisk on full speed until stiff and looking like clouds. Add the sugar, one teaspoonful at a time, still whisking at full speed until it has all been added. Blend the cornflour and white wine vinegar together in a small bowl and fold into the meringue mixture.

Spoon the mixture into the circle marked on the non-stick baking parchment on the baking tray and spread out gently so that the meringue forms a 23cm (9") circle, building the sides up well so that they are higher than the middle.

Bake in the simmering oven for about $1\frac{1}{2}$ hours or until firm to the touch and the meringue comes away from the paper easily.

Carefully remove the meringue from the baking tray, peeling off the baking parchment and slide it onto a flat serving plate. Mix the whipped cream and yoghurt together in a bowl. Mix half the fruit with the cream and yoghurt and spoon into the centre of the pavlova, decorate with the remaining fruits. Leave in the fridge for about 1 hour before serving.

serves 8

conventional oven
Pre-heat the oven to 160C/140C Fan/Gas 3. Place the meringue in the oven but immediately reduce the temperature to 150C/130C Fan/Gas 2. Bake for about $1\frac{1}{2}$ hours until firm to the touch and a pale beige colour. Turn off the oven and leave the meringue in the oven to become quite cold.

lush strawberry cheesecake

Use ripe full flavoured strawberries for this wonderfully fresh tasting chilled summer cheesecake. No gelatine or raw eggs – so simple. You can substitute the strawberries with raspberries. Fantastic served (as illustrated) with Crimson Fruit Compote (p181).

❄ Not suitable for freezing.

base
8 Hobnob biscuits
2 tablespoons Demerara sugar
25g (1oz) butter

filling
400g (14oz) ripe strawberries
1 x 250g (9oz) tub mascarpone cheese
50g (2oz) caster sugar
150 ml ($\frac{1}{4}$ pint) double cream, whipped
2 tablespoons lemon juice

Grease a 20cm (8") spring form or loose bottomed tin. Line the base with a disc of parchment paper and the sides with clingfilm.

Put the biscuits into a poly bag, bash with a rolling pin or base of a saucepan until fine crumbs, tip into a bowl and stir in the sugar. Measure the butter into a pan and heat on the simmering plate until the butter has melted, stir in the crumbs. Press into the base of the tin and leave to chill while you make the filling.

Reserve 175g (6oz) of strawberries, keeping the tops on for decoration. Hull the remaining and whiz in a processor until smooth. Add the mascarpone, sugar and lemon juice to the processor and whiz again until smooth. Pour into a bowl.

Whip the cream until just stiff, pour the strawberry mixture into a bowl and carefully mix together until smooth. Spoon into the tin and level the top. Chill in the fridge for minimum of 2 hours to set.

To serve, decorate the set cheesecake with slices of the reserved strawberries. Serve chilled.

serves 6–8

conventional oven
Warm the butter in a pan on the hob.

mango mousse in minutes

I challenge you to find a quicker mousse than this one. You can replace the mango with other fruits, but make sure you add 300 ml of fruit to the mousse mixture. Can be made up to 24 hours ahead. Goes perfectly with Orange Shortbread biscuits (p180). I sometimes garnish with a sprig of fresh mint.

❄ Not suitable for freezing.

3 large mangoes, peeled, cut into cubes
2 tablespoons icing sugar
300ml (½ pint) double cream
2 egg whites

You will need 6 large wine glasses.

Whiz the mango and icing sugar in a blender or processor until smooth. Reserve 300 ml (½ pint) of the purée to mix with the mousse. Keep the remainder separate to go on top of the mousse.

Whisk the cream into soft peaks. Fold in the reserved 300ml of mango purée to the cream. Whisk the egg whites until stiff and fold into the cream mixture until smooth.

Spoon the mousse into six wine glasses. Spoon the reserved mango purée on top of the mousse. Transfer to the fridge to firm up for at least 2 hours.

Serve straight from the fridge.

serves 6

orange shortbread

Traditional butter shortbread with orange zest. The semolina gives it a lovely crunch but you could use cornflour instead.

❄ Freezes well

175g (6 oz) plain flour
175g (6 oz) butter, at room temperature
75g (3 oz) caster sugar
75g (3 oz) semolina
rind of one orange, finely grated

topping
25g (1oz) Demerara sugar

Measure the flour, caster sugar, butter and semolina into a processor and mix until thoroughly combined and comes together to form a dough consistency. (This can also be done by hand by rubbing the butter into the flour first, then adding the sugar and semolina and working the ingredients together to form a ball of mixture.) Add the orange rind so it is evenly combined.

Press the shortbread into the small Aga roasting tin and level with the back of a spoon until even. Sprinkle the top with the Demerara sugar.

2-oven AGA
Bake on the lowest set of runners in the roasting oven, with the cold sheet on the second set of runners for about 20 minutes or until pale golden. Transfer to simmering oven for a further 45 minutes until firm.

3- and 4-oven AGA
Slide onto the lowest set of runners in the baking oven for about 45 minutes until pale golden and firm. If getting too brown slide the cold sheet on the second set of runners.

Allow the shortbread to cool in the tin for a few minutes then cut six across the long side and four across the short side to give you 24 fingers. Carefully lift the shortbread fingers out of the tin with a small palette knife and leave to cool completely on a wire rack. Store in an airtight tin.

makes 24 shortbread fingers

conventional oven
Pre-heat the oven to 160C/140C/Gas 3. Spread the mixture into a traybake tin 33cm x 23cm (12" x 9"). Bake in the pre-heated oven for about 30–40 minutes until the shortbread is a pale golden and cooked through.

crimson fruit compote

This is delicious at any time of day - perfect when served cold at breakfast with yoghurt or when served warm as a dessert after lunch or dinner with cream or crème fraîche.

❄ Not suitable for freezing.

4 tablespoons Ribena cordial
4 tablespoons water
50g (2oz) caster sugar
300g (10 oz) blueberries
2 just ripe nectarines or peaches, each sliced into 8 wedges
150g (5oz) raspberries

Measure all the ingredients, except the raspberries into a wide-based saucepan.

Heat on the simmering plate, stirring until the sugar has dissolved. Boil for about 4–5 minutes until the liquid has thickened slightly. Stir in the raspberries and spoon into a serving dish.

serves 4

conventional oven
Simmer over a low heat, stirring until the sugar has dissolved. Boil for a couple of minutes to thicken the liquid.

index

a

b

c

acknowledgements

Firstly, a special thank you to lovely Lucinda Kaizik – this is the second book Lucinda has helped me with and I am forever grateful for her dedication, professionalism and laughter... Lucinda you are a treasure, thank you.

Of course, big thanks to Jon Croft at Absolute Press who asked me to write this book, Meg and Matt too – it has been an absolute (pardon the pun!) joy working with you, thank you for believing in me. The photography in this book is stunning, all thanks to Philip Webb, I could not have dreamt for better photos, thank you.

Thank you to Laura James, for such amazing support and Dawn Roads and the team at Aga. My agent Michele Topham who once again has guided me through the 'being an author' process! Also to Linda Shanks and Fiona Lindsey at Limelight Management for taking me on.

My wonderful family, my parents, brothers, sister-in-laws, nieces and nephews for being chief tasters, and for all your support and encouragement that I can reach a deadline in one piece! You are the world to me. My wonderful friends for fun, laughter and seeing me through another book, always supporting me in every way, you know that life wouldn't be life without you all.

And finally, but with all my love, to my friend Mary Berry; Mary we are a team forever and a day, thank you for your unreserved support, encouragement and belief in me – words will never thank you enough.

Thank you and much love.